M000102779

✪✪✪✪✪

"This book is a wonderful read. Reilly deals with the serious topic of religion through the ages and the problem of dogma with a refreshing dose of both wit and sarcasm. For all those who are looking for an alternative to organized religion and authoritarian dogma but nonetheless believe in a higher power, We Are the Post-Theological offers an inspiring roadmap for the future."

—C. Heidelberg, Seattle

✪✪✪✪✪

"This book is more than timely. It skewers the existing religious establishment while providing a new home for the religiously un-affiliated. It is a book that everyone who questions their religion should read."

—J. Khatri, Mumbai

✪✪✪✪✪

"I had no idea that I was Post-Theological until I read Steve's book. "Spiritual but not religious" doesn't really communicate my true beliefs but this book helped me clarify them. I now feel like part of a larger community with common shared beliefs and sense of belonging. Enlightening!"

—M. Green, Sydney

✪✪✪✪✪

"Written with agility, strengthened with testimonials and real-life experiences, Steve Reilly brings our feet back on earth while keeping our head in the sky. With spirituality (and sometimes sarcasm), he questions clergies, interpreters of the Book(s), faith manipulators and deciphers how dogmas and their mechanisms do shackle minds and free will with their paradoxes.

Steve embarks us on a journey towards a clearer mind and little more wisdom, and yes, for the Free Man, the Theological milestone is behind. A must read!"

—A. Nessali, Lyon

WE ARE THE POST-THEOLOGICAL

*A SLIGHTLY HUMOROUS AND DEEPLY
SERIOUS EXPLANATION OF THE FASTEST
GROWING RELIGIOUS GROUP*

BY
STEVE REILLY

Copyright © A Pulp Non-Fiction Publication, 2020

All rights reserved. No part of this publication may be reproduced, stored in
a retrieval system, or transmitted in any form or by any means, mechanical,
photocopying, recording or otherwise, without prior permission in writing of the
author.

ISBN: 1735063819 (paperback)

For Christopher Hitchens

May You Rest in Peace in your empty atheistic non-existence!

ACKNOWLEDGEMENTS

I want to give credit to the great thinkers, writers, and literature that informed this book. My search for purpose goes back to my teen years, so it is possible I don't remember all who helped build this book's foundation. For those who I neglect to mention, please forgive me.

Those I do remember include Peter Michael Boyd, Sam Harris, Richard Dawkins, Christopher Hitchens, William Shermer, Cynthia Heidelberg, Willian Lane Craig, the Dali Lama, Lao Tzu, "Rocket" Rodney Lane, Jesus Christ, the Gautama Buddha, the writers of the Bhagavad Gita, the writers of the Bible, the Book of Mormon, the Tao Te Ching, the teachings of the Buddha, YouTube, the Pew Research Center for Religion and the contributors to Wikipedia.

As I read, listened, and observed them throughout my life, they made me think and question my most basic beliefs about humanity.

And like the song says, "That's what it's all about."

TABLE OF CONTENTS

AUTHOR'S NOTE

As the reader, you will notice several grammatical peculiarities in this book. I want to explain the reasoning behind them so you don't mistake them for poor editing or lack of grammatical knowledge on my part.

The first is my intentional use of lower-case letters in religious titles, terms, and supreme entities throughout the book, except for *Post-Theological*. While I do capitalize the first letters of religious persons like Jesus and Mohammed, I deliberately neglect to do the same for god, allah, yahweh, and all three major monotheisms: judaism, christianity, and islam. I intend to make it obvious that I do not extend any more importance to these words than they deserve.

To some, this will seem disrespectful, and it may indeed put them off. But they are not this book's intended audience, and my grammatical faux pas are in keeping with the content and context of my arguments regarding religion. As for my deliberate double capitalization of the term Post-Theological, I do this to irritate the sanctimonious theocratic cognoscenti.

While the term Post-Theological is usually used as an adjective, I use it as a noun to emphasize the term's importance as a belief and movement. Just as we use catholic, protestant, muslim, and jew as nouns, I extend that honor to the Post-Theological.

This brings me to my second point.

As I watch the New Atheists and Theologians debate on various media, YouTube, talk shows, in books and magazines, with few exceptions (perhaps Lawrence Krauss), they take themselves riously. Their lack of humor makes them tough to read and even tougher to listen to. I use humor and satire to make and enhance points and poke fun at their faux gravitas. This is not in any way to disrespect any one person – I disrespect religion – not people.

But since we are on the subject, let's talk about respect or rather the lack of it by the so-called religious.

People like my father (a devout catholic who feels the pedophilia church scandal was a small blip on the otherwise noble history of his church) will undoubtedly feel as though I am disrespectful in criticizing and laying bare the immoral and untenable dogma of their faith. I expect the same condemnation from jews, muslims, evangelicals, and perhaps even wiccans (yeah, right, like that's a real religion).

But their outrage in inherently hypocritical.

This book will most offend those who readily condemn anyone not a member of their own proprietary church. People like my father easily and without guilt, condemn every other religion with righteous certainty and "moral clarity." He will tell you that their followers are misguided and doomed to eternal damnation. Those who believe theirs is the "one, true religion" defend it to their core and seek to destroy anyone and anything that might threaten it. Christians ignore other religions' great art and achievements as not-quite-equal to those created by the christian church. They do not believe that muslims or jews can feel deeper wonder from the progress achieved by their great leaders than they do of the christian artists and thinkers.

Many if not most western historians believe western civilization *is* history and everything else, just a bunch of also-rans. Western elitism (read christianity) rejects eastern history, art, and culture as sub-par lacking the great Western thinkers' sophistication and intelligence.

So, let's cut with the bullshit.

My critique of your religion does not give you the special right to be outraged that someone dared point out the all-to-evident flaws in your theological ideology; neither you nor your religion is special or above criticism. Just as you dismiss every other belief system in the world except your own, I dismiss yours. My dismissiveness towards your church is not in any way different from your dismissiveness of other faiths. So, get over your theological narcissism and join the modern world, asshole.

Whew... that felt good.

Finally, I'd like to also address the absence of an annotated bibliography and footnotes in my book. In my life-long research for this tome, I used some specific texts like the Teachings of the Buddha, the Bible, the Hadiths, the Quran and Hadiths, and the Bhagavat Gita. But when it comes to modern-day religion and philosophy, I found more modern-day sources like YouTube and recent reputable independent studies and surveys to be the best source of real-time discourse and debate between the theological and anti-theological.

However, I have read and re-read several books from the New Atheists, including Christopher Hitchens's *God Is Not Great*, Sam Harris's *The End of Faith* and Dawkin's *The God Delusion* and all of the major tomes that form the foundation and starting point for the primary monotheisms; judaism (The Torah) christianity (The new and old testaments) and islam (The Qu 'ran). The significant books from eastern religions and philosophies also helped form and develop this book's main thesis, including the Tao Te Ching, The Bhagavad Gita, and the Teaching of the Buddha.

When I use a quote from one of these great thinkers or writers, I give them credit in the narrative. I hope and trust that is enough for the reader.

With the exception of the Pew Research on Religion and Public Life Project as the foundation of my claims on most religious metrics, most of the other thoughts are my own.

PREFACE

Why I am not a christian or anything else for that matter.

My mother has a quote I both love and hate. Whenever she encountered criticism of her catholic parenting approach, her retort was always the same, "There's nothing wrong with guilt and shame. They helped me raise my children, and they're all fine."

I love this defense of her parenting skills because I understand her loving intentions to raise her children to be good and moral adults. I hate it because her confident reliance on catholic and christian principles to raise her children is the foundation of the neurotic and emotional struggles I've dealt with all my life.

So, in case you are wondering, yes, I have this thing against religion.

Raised in a catholic household, educated in a catholic grade school and high school, and having attended an Augustinian University, you might think my anger at religion comes from being physically and metaphorically bludgeoned by the Baltimore Catechism or from being forced to sit through boring and pointless religion classes in my sixteen years of theological education. But that is not the reason for my animosity towards religious systems of belief.

My bias against organized religion comes from the writings, preaching and practices of priests, nuns, popes, mullahs, rabbis and other religious leaders I have encountered, served and studied under and over for many years.

I remember clearly the first-time religious dogma troubled me.

I was in third grade, and Sister Honorata (actual name) was teaching the innocents about heaven. She explained that if we were good, meaning that we followed the Commandments, we would experience blissful happiness in a place where our every desire is fulfilled. That the reward for being a good, observant catholic will be eternal life in a billowy, transcendent land.

This literally scared the shit out of me.

Spending eternity in any one place, regardless of how heavenly it was, seemed like a nightmare. I was already so bored from listening to nuns that there was no way I could wrap my head around being anywhere or doing anything for eternity.

I was convinced that if I had to live forever, I'd kill myself.

Then there were the milk bottles.

These metaphors for a soul represented how sinful you were; the more you sinned, the darker your milk bottle; white, gray, and black. Catholic clergy and nuns used the milk bottle metaphor to terrify small children into behaving. While your soul was never completely white (Original Sin turned it a color similar to nude hosiery), it became progressively darker until completely black as you committed sins against the Father.

One horrible fear that haunted me constantly was that if my bottle was completely black from mortal sin, and I was to die, even by accident, it would damn my soul to the fires of hell. And the only way for me to avoid this horrible fate was the opportunity to confess my sins to a priest and do my assigned penance.

Now imagine a *really, really* terrified child being *really, really* careful walking to church every Saturday evening for the particularly catholic sacrament of Confession. Fearing for my eternal life, I was hyper-vigilant to make sure I wasn't run over by a car before reaching the warm and comfortable kneeling pad in the confessional box. That would mean being condemned to the fires of hell, which, if you'd been exposed to any Hieronymus Bosch paintings, didn't look like a fun place to spend any time, let alone the rest of it.

As a child, I spent most of my life in fear of being punished by this god son-of-a-bitch. You see, the nuns and priests taught children the theological cause and effect theory of sinning. It goes like this: If you sin, god punishes you, either in this life or the next If you are good, he rewards you in this life or next. Either way, there is no avoiding his celestial accountability.

God will make sure you are punished now or in the future no matter the extenuating circumstances, no matter the excuse, no matter the crime. You are going to get it; it is only a matter of time. It isn't even necessary for you to commit the crime to warrant punishment. Thought Crime was just as real as Real Crime. You think the act and your bottle gets darker. And since this god knows and sees all, there is no way out of this wash cycle of sin-guilt-punishment and repeat until clean.

If you combine this spiritual cause-and-effect with typical youth behaviors and sexual urges, you inevitably end up being punished for falling short of unattainable expectations. As an adolescent, whenever I happened to steal, lie, or think of nakedness (which was most of the time), I thought the next bad thing that happened was personal retribution from my god. (Thus, the inherent narcissism of religion – to believe I would have a god paying so much attention to my behavior, especially when naked. Thank you, Christopher H).

This contorted belief had both its terrifying and soothing aspects. When I did something wrong, I lived in anxious anticipation of the punishment about to rain down on me by my "all-merciful" god. But when the next bad thing happened, I felt relief as if a cross had been lifted (pun intended).

But if I could get to Saturday night confession and convince myself and the priest that I was sincere, I would be forgiven with a couple of Hail Mary's and an Our Father – a small price to pay for looking at Playboy magazines and filching candy from the local drug store if you think about it. Once forgiven, I would be off to sin again for the week.

Side note: I firmly believe the catholic sacrament of Confession contributed to the church's pedophile/child rape crimes. (Really? A once-a-week reset button?)

I took this to a bizarre and inevitable extreme when, as a young man, my sexual urges terrified me. Because of the all-too-catholic fear of sex and anything sexual (this is where it gets more universal), my sexual thoughts were crimes enough, but doing anything to satisfy my adolescent cravings ensured my milk bottle would turn into a black-hole-of-a-milk-bottle sucking in any hope of my redemption.

But... being a healthy teen with a god-given libido and sex drive, I found the urge overwhelming and at times succumbed to my weaknesses.

It so happened that one rainy autumn Saturday morning, I awoke feeling randy and made a trip into the bathroom for some enjoyable self-abuse. (How did we come to describe a completely human act with this term?) When finished, I felt the inevitable guilt and dread creep over me as I awaited my own private wrath of god.

This particular morning was different in a very terrible way, however.

No sooner had I returned to my warm bed when my mother rushed crying into my room with the news that my father's best friend had lost control of his car on wet leaves, crashed into a tree, and died. My sin-guilt-shame logic put two and two together; I'd killed Dad's best friend by masturbating.

This episode would be hilariously funny if it weren't so horribly painful.

This may seem crazy and debilitatingly painful, but when I think of other horrible things that happened in my own catholic parish, I got off easy.

I had an elementary school friend who experienced the unjust and crushing judgment of religion at its most evil. The Fleming twins were benign troublemakers at my grade school, Saint Philomena's, in Philadelphia. One day Paul, the more rambunctious of the twins, found himself in front of our fifth-grade classroom as the focus of Sister Alma Dolores's (once again, actual name) anger for not paying attention. In his attempt to avoid her swings with a heavy, thick, wood-and-silver banded ruler, he got his foot tangled in the jumbo-sized rosary beads that served as a belt over the nun's tunic (a must-have accessory for a bride of the lord, as the good nuns described themselves).

Paul leaped out of harm's way in one swift move and the jumbo rosary swept Sister Dolores's feet out from under her, causing her to fall heavily to the floor. The sound of a crack didn't bode well for anyone, especially Paul. Sister Alma Dolores had broken her hip. She was transferred to the hospital by ambulance, and while being treated, contracted a deadly infection and succumbed.

From that day forward The Fleming family was cursed, shamed, and shunned forever by our parish clergy, nuns, and flock. The family was never again able to worship, go to school, or do anything as a parish member as they were outcast and black-balled. The parish forever banned these poor victims of a terrible but innocent accident.

The horrible post-script to this story is that a year later, Paul's twin accidentally set himself on fire while playing with a cigarette lighter and died from his burns. Rather than compassion from the religious community, the priests and nuns proclaimed it an act of god in punishment for the family's evil ways. Even after their tragedy, they still refused to let the Fleming family back into the fold.

So much for christian fucking empathy.

Some readers may think I was an overly impressionable and confused youth. When I was growing up, catholicism was taught the old way with cracking rulers and bleeding knuckles. The nuns at St. Philomena's threatened to tie kids to a post in the "subtu'um" (a made-up faux Latin word that was basically the basement under the convent) to let the rats chew at their feet until they died if they didn't behave (I think nuns got away with way more stuff when I was a kid).

But I was brought up with the same tenets, laws, and commandments as any religion, albeit with different emphasis and maybe lacking the total nun-thing. But you get my point.

My struggles with catholic dogma have all the universal elements common to major religions: the idea that an invisible god watches us all the time and sees everything we do, that we need only think of committing the sin to be punished, that we are set-up by a god that gives us free will but uses a carrot or stick to get us to do the "right" things, that there is an inevitable reckoning at the end of life that allows us to bask in god's heaven or burn in his hell.

It's all the same.

The strange thing is that despite the problems I've had with monotheisms, I still have a very strong faith. Not faith in a god per se, or a divine invisible man but faith that there is more than we can ever know. That there is a reason for life and a purpose to the universe. Religious dogma may have destroyed my faith in catholicism, but it never shook my faith in a divine hand.

When my daughters reached a certain age, each asked me about religion. Prompted by conversations at their schools, they wanted to know whether we were protestant, catholic, jewish, or other religious groups. Being a father who believes that children are much smarter than we give them credit for, and that teaching children ideology limits their learning (including political and cultural), I told my girls about the world's religions.

I explained the basic christian tenets and commandments and about Jesus Christ and his teachings. I did the same for judaism, islam, hinduism and buddhism, providing them as much background as I knew with as much objectivity as I could. I let them know that I would support whatever belief they felt resonated with them.

My younger daughter decided she is a christian because she likes the baby Jesus. That is as good a reason as any and better than many. My older daughter didn't really settle on a particular belief, at least not at the time; perhaps she will as she gets older. It doesn't matter; I love them for who they are, not what they believe.

Over time, it was inevitable that they'd asked me about my beliefs. I was honest, explaining that while I did not believe in a specific religion, I had a very strong faith in god. I explained that something makes me feel as though there is more to the universe than the reality we see every day. My oldest asked if I could believe in god without being part of a religion. Of course, it is possible, I told her. Why wouldn't it be? Her logical next question was, "Well, if you're not a christian, a jew, or something else, what would you call yourself?"

"I don't know," I said.

I am a moral person. I contribute to the poor, raise my children to be honest, respectful, and grateful, and try hard to be a good friend, son, brother, and father. I am grateful for everything I have – not grateful to a god, but grateful that I am alive with a healthy, happy family and make pretty good money. While I was not sure of my religion's name, I was sure of a number of things.

After much thought, reading, and therapy, I broke free of my religions' Bronze Age myths, lies, and rules written in crumbling books supposedly penned by our creator. It became impossible for me to sideline my logic, and blindly believe in things that no longer made sense in my world. I could no longer put faith in any religion that believes an invisible man watches my every move, judging and meting out punishment in some sort of moral balancing act.

I cannot.

It always struck me as dumb that people could unquestioningly believe something that the other half of the world's population did not, all the while knowing that the other half has the same amount of religious surety in their faith. All religions believe that their "moral certainty" is superior to any other.

For me, letting go of christianity's "moral certainty" and other religion's claim to the same moral clarity allowed me to embrace the ambiguity and wonder of life. This has brought me great freedom and peace.

I no longer feel guilty for things I am not, nor ever could be considered responsible for. I do not feel shame for being a male of my species, and I do not feel shame for being attracted to my species' female members. I no longer believe that one day I will stand before a god in judgment to be taken up to a cloudy heaven or shoved down into an endless pit of fire and brimstone. I no longer believe an all-knowing god acts in any personal way to make sure I stay on the straight and narrow. I no longer believe in the concept of original sin.

I know many who feel the same.

Many are fed up with shame and guilt. Many are done with organized religions' sclerotic dogma and shame-filled judgments. Many are done with feeling guilty for being male, for being female, for being human.

We, the Post-Theological, are done with the ancient rules that try to dictate our actions and feelings.

We are done listening to old men preach old beliefs from the pulpits, mosques, and temples.

We are done with the Iron Age baggage of misogynistic and repressive teachings.

We are done with the "interpretations" of god's words by holy men with their own agendas.

We reject the idea that there is one true religion.

We reject that we can know what god wants from us. We reject the idea that god has a personal interest in our actions.

We reject the idea of everlasting life in a glorious heaven or horrible hell.

We reject the idea that religion is the only source of morality.

We reject the idea that man is guilty of Original Sin or flawed and in need of redemption.

We believe.

As the Post-Theological, we believe in an extra-universal force that we can never know.

We believe that life – all life – is precious, not for religious reasons but for the sheer joy of being alive against incredibly bad universal odds.

We believe in moral truth as a by-product of evolution and necessary for the continuation of our species.

We believe that men and women of all religions, races, ethnicities, and countries are intellectually, economically, politically, and morally equal and should be treated that way.

We believe in freedom; freedom of speech, freedom of religion, freedom from fear, and freedom from want. We believe in one-person/one-vote.

We believe that humans thrive better in humanistic, egalitarian, secular societies, and governments.

We are the Post-Theological, and we are proud of our faith.

INTRODUCTION

After a millennium of checkered existence, religion as we know it is finally running out of gas... thank god.

Today, the number of people who affiliate themselves with a specific religious denomination is declining across the globe. Humans are beginning to realize that the simple answers provided by their Iron Age religious beliefs no longer adequately address the more complex questions raised by our expanding knowledge of the universe. Our world's complexity no longer allows for blind faith in ancient texts; we cannot take the teachings of old prophets as a foundation for our lives.

Curiously enough, concurrent with the decline in religious affiliation, is the increasing number of people believing in a divine entity. Current research shows that while attachments to religious institutions are in decline, the number of people who believe there is someone or something at the cosmic controls is growing.

This divergence of beliefs reflects the gap between past religious thinking and the unfolding of the next theological paradigm as yet unformed and unclear. The world's increasing sophistication of thought and spread of knowledge results in less reason or need to commit to a specific dogmatic doctrine. This Post-Theological paradigm is the natural evolution of religion, the next step in religious thought.

Much like Galileo, our deeper knowledge allows us to see through these archaic, medieval religious beliefs (I am talking to you catholics... heaven, hell, purgatory and limbo – really?) to develop a more transparent view of the universe. The population of earth is learning at an ever-increasingly rate, and that learning is spreading faster than at any time in the history of humanity. We are getting smarter.

Today, even a pre-teen African child with a cell phone has access to all the information humans have accumulated since human thought and writing began. This incredible distribution of information, history, opinions, and news at light speed creates an egalitarian and, albeit at times, biased foundation of thought for all humans on the planet.

This unprecedented expansion of knowledge creates more questions for this young African child (and us) than it gives answers. The good news is that these questions destroy the power religion uses to control people. Being told that spirits and demons occupy the jungle makes about the same amount of sense to that African child as does that an all-knowing invisible man in the sky watches us and our every move.

This trend towards challenging the theological status quo will continue to accelerate. As we acquire more and more experience and knowledge, we will inevitably continue to outgrow our need for the simple answers religion provides for our much more complex questions. The planet has and continues to progress towards a more secular world. The arc of history bends toward greater knowledge and lesser fundamentalism at times at a glacial pace, but still, it bends.

Today's religious fundamentalisms, both Eastern and Western, are the death throes of modern dogma. The headline catching acts of violence by evangelical and conservative sects do not make their religious tenets more valid or palatable. From radical islam to orthodox judaism, the fringe cannot hold the center.

Popes have outlived their usefulness, mullahs rail against ghosts, and yogis "detach" from the world to save it. Even allowing for the fact that people become more religious as they get older and that some religions seem to be gaining momentum (specifically radical islam in the last ten years and christian evangelism in the last twenty), statistics on religious affiliation show an accelerating decline in people's connection to organized religious institutions.

The human religious trajectory started with the worship of the stars, moon, sun, and seasons. It will end with the acceptance that religious dogma serves only the purposes of those who write or "interpret" the words of their god; when people accept that there is no word of god to interpret because he/she/it speaks a language we can never understand.

One of the many reasons humans continue to cling to religion is because so many assumptions about our world are being challenged and debunked. Each day our ever-evolving science uncovers more and more that doesn't make sense to our Newtonian view of the world. The universe does not work like a big clock that we can eventually figure out. New and unexpected discoveries explode the foundational assumptions that built our view of the world from Newtonian physics to quantum theory as we push the envelope of science. Religion attempts to provide us with a predictable and unquestioned understanding of a world that is becoming less predictable, generating more questions every day.

Debunking the long-lasting belief that the world was flat or that the sun revolved around the earth had incredible effects on our species. From our modern vantage point, it is difficult to comprehend the impact prompted by these discoveries we today do not question. These discoveries had huge impacts on society, culture, and religion and fundamentally changed the way people view themselves, their world, and their god.

As we leave our ancestors' religion behind, I hope Post-Theological thought will have a huge impact on the world and how we live our lives.

1

POST-THEOLOGICAL FAITH

"It's hard to dance with the devil on your back, so shake him off."
Florence and the Machine

The post-modern dilemma faced by the Post-Theological is the challenge of reconciling Bronze and Iron Age theologies with the reality of modern life. Most religions have their origins in a time of near-Neanderthal human evolution. From a historical standpoint, islam is the "newest" major religion founded by Mohammed about 600 years after the death of Jesus Christ. The rest are more than two thousand years old.

Before the foundation of the first monotheisms, people worshiped bears, bulls, fire, horses, the sun, the moon, and almost anything else you could put on an elevated platform, including golden calves. The foundational tomes of each major religion were written by people who could not understand or comprehend the meteorological or natural phenomena they encountered every day. Ancient religion was used as a way for miserable people to cope with a miserable existence. Prayer and sacrifice were the spiritual tools to ask a merciful (you would hope) god to improve crop yields, stave off the plague, and heal the unhealable.

It would be nice to think that one day everyone woke up with a new perspective on religion or the idea that god is a singular person/being in their heads. But before monotheism, most religions were animistic, believing that all things were imbued with a spiritual essence. It is easy to see how today's religions have rituals and rites evolved from their animistic lineage. Every religion stole, hijacked, and appropriated animistic beliefs and rituals that predated their proprietary belief system. The origins of almost all religion's "holy days" can be traced to pagan societies and their calendar of important milestones. Instead of fighting the entrenched holidays and important meteorological events to establish their own identity, it was simply easier to lay their "non-pagan" calendar over the ones that already existed.

It is difficult, if not impossible, to connect the dots that tie the birth of Jesus Christ to December 25th. Most likely, Jesus was born in the spring or summer as shepherds tending to their flocks is not something anyone would be doing in Jerusalem in late December. Pope Julius I declared Christmas December 25th to replace the roman celebration of Saturnalia, which featured an orgy at the Temple of Saturn, wild pagan festivities, and even some "gag gift" giving (the origins of secret Santa, I guess). Lupercalia was an ancient celebration that occurred on February 15th. The christian church appropriated the day before to create the birthday of the supposed Saint Valentine. And while islam holy days do not tie directly to any pagan holidays, it is curious to note that Yom Kippur and Ramadan would fall in the same week if the islamic and jewish calendars were the same. While offshoots, movements, and sects like mormonism in christianity, conservative orthodox in judaism, and the muslim brotherhood in islam all began in the modern era, the foundational teachings are based on literature and lore from as late as AD 650 to earlier than 1300 BC.

More and more, the Post-Theological find it hard to continue to believe the primitive dogma re-espoused by theocratic leaders in our hyper-modern world of technology, globalization, and financial connectivity. Watching old men preach old lies from old pulpits leaves me/us with a disconnect between the myths and superstitions of ancient religions and the wondrous scientific revelations we learn daily about our mystical universe. The cognitive dissonance between the reality we experience and expand every day and the sclerotic, dogmatic preaching of long-winded holy (or is it holey?) men leaves many with spiritual emptiness.

In the West, some fill this spiritual chasm by turning to Eastern philosophy/religion. The late-onset adoption of buddhism by western peoples is questionable if not cynical attempt to fill a void created by the hyper-capitalism to which the west seems addicted.

The western world has, to some extent, fetishized buddhism and other eastern sects into almost caricatures of their original teachings. In my old Seattle neighborhood, almost every week, a new buddhist temple or Ashram opens. This appropriation of eastern thought into "quasi-spiritualism" is as cynical and shallow as the religions it replaces. It is curious, if not alarming that New Age gurus interpret the eastern philosophy and writings to fit their agendas and then cherry-pick the tenets that most fit their narcissistic creed to entice the spiritually nomadic into giving their lives and money to the cause. (Talking to you, Deepak.)

And even though eastern religions are seen by many as the antidote to western superficiality and hyper-capitalism, while less dogmatic and structured, their focus on another less autocratic set of rules and "right ways" still fall within the rubric of organized religion and common dogma. The idea of reincarnation up or down the food chain is nice to contemplate, but it is still a wild-ass guess.

Buddhist monks claim they can identify the reincarnation of past buddhas in today's society. But the last time they proclaimed a young Spanish boy, Osel Hita Torres as the true reincarnated inheritor of the buddhist leadership, he turned his back on them.

Currently, he is studying film in Madrid and trying very hard to hide from the enigmatic order.

And despite their serene leaders and humanistic beliefs, followers still seem drawn into the same political and social conflicts as the rest of us monotheists.

Other spiritually disenfranchised monotheists try to fill the resulting emptiness by denying it exists at all. The rise and precipitous fall in popularity of the New Atheists and their godless worldview indicate that people are still entertaining alternative ideas if not converting to their anti-theistic vision of the world.

While the nihilistic view of the New Atheists may be an answer to some, it ultimately leaves most still searching for meaning and purpose in a Post-Theological world. The populist writings of Sam Harris, Christopher Hitchens, Richard Dawkins, and Daniel Bennet, often referred to as the Four Horsemen of Atheism had their fifteen minutes of fame. While interesting and lively, they offered only pedantic and nihilistic screeds condescending to anyone who might dare to believe in anything, let alone an invisible godhead.

Optimistically, many who fully think through their atheist dogma are unwilling to embrace the idea of no-god. This is evident in the short half-life of the New Atheists' popularity in the last decade. Once thought to be the answer and new home to the spiritual seeker, their movement's growth has slowed and is in decline.

This rapid arc may be due to the overtly "evangelical atheism," which condemned all religious believers as fools at best and murderers at worst. They could not see a problem calling Timothy McVeigh the instigator of the Oklahoma City bombing, a "christian terrorist," even though his motivations were obviously political. The New Atheists' tendency to ignore social and political pressures by grouping Tehran, Hamas, and the PLO as "religious extremists" is a simple and shallow statement based on their evangelical-like attempts to build an atheist movement.

Then there are the true charlatans, New Age preachers who use pseudoscience "woo-woo", pushing us to new heights of self-absorption while promoting their brand of "fast-food enlighten-ment" on YouTube. These semi-certified gurus (yes, I am talking to you again, Deepak) who proselytize about nonlocal, spiritual, universal consciousness while cashing in at their local banks only leave us more cynical. The idea that we are one with the universe is as self-absorbed as any faith. The universe does not care about us, and the belief that reality only exists in our perception is a simple human conceit.

There is an overabundance of self-promoting new-age "think-ers" in the west who appropriate or create their own "mini-re-ligion," drawing in the insecure and spiritually nomadic. The list includes wiccans (there is no test to determine if you are a witch, you need only proclaim yourself one), the neopagans like the Church of All Worlds (American cult founded in 1962), the Church of Aphrodite (started by a Long Island Russian emigre in 1939 with one goddess) and Lectorium Rosicrianum, founded in 1924, teaches the concept of the human being as a microcosm of the world made up of visible and invisible vehicles surrounded by a magnetic field and bounded by a microcosmic firmament. (Don't ask, don't fucking ask.) Even though most of these pseudo-theologies are benign, at times, we end up with a group like the Heaven's Gate cult. The founder and loon-in-chief, Marshall Applewhite, claimed that he came from a different dimension (which he didn't) on a mission from outer space (which he wasn't) and had to return to his planet (which didn't exist). He convinced 39 spiritual nomads to believe in him so devoutly that they com-mitted mass suicide to initiate the trip back to "whence they came" (which they didn't).

It is understandable that with all of the ambiguity and change in the modern world, spiritual emptiness can become so deep it motivates some to seek solace in extremely dysfunctional and illogical movements. Think of how over the years, mainstream looney religions have become accepted, including scientology (We descend from clams? Really?), mormonism (they want to change it to LDS because of the you-know, the polygamy thing), jehovah witnesses (no blood transfusions and no celebrating any pagan-based holidays including Christmas). in response to a world that at times can seem to be coming unhinged, people turn to these gods of false certainty. The need for something to believe in is a natural human desire.

In ancient times, the frightened masses sought to make sense of confusing and potentially life-threatening natural occurrences in an often random and violent world. Life in those times was more difficult than any of us can imagine; surviving until the ripe old age of 32 was an accomplishment in the time of Jesus. Finding a purpose to live when most of your children didn't live past the age of two, when your friends and family most likely died in a petty war or succumbed to infection often brought on by rotting, aching teeth was just too much to ask. A simple, painless death was enough of a reward in a life that was "brutal, painful and thankfully short."

Today, while most of us will avoid a brutish death, we still search for meaning and purpose in a life and world that can be very difficult to grasp. The search for the meaning of life in a world where "life, liberty, and the pursuit of happiness" is enshrined in founding documents is a different quest than our ancient forebearers took up. It was natural that the ancient's beliefs in animism and other paganisms supplied a rationale for the terrifying randomness of life in the time when humans were, for the most part, still considered "prey" by other animals. But we need to outgrow our adolescent theological systems and stupid self- and other-serving dogmatic religious beliefs.

Today's search is no different. The false gods of christianity, judaism, islam, and other beliefs have run their course. The ancients sacrificed their children in the hope of warding off the plague or being rewarded with a good growing season. But even they tired of the emptiness offered by these exploitive and smugly self-confident snake oil vendors. The masses are searching for something else, and the data shows it.

A recent Pew Research Religion & Public Life Project survey shows that Unaffiliated Believers, those who claim no allegiance to any religion, make up more than 16 percent of the world's population. The only religions that make up more of the global population than the Unaffiliated are christians at 31 percent and muslims at 23 percent. Christianity has declined 12 percentage points in the US in the last ten years, and as of October 2019, the "nones," which include atheist, agnostic, or "nothing in particular," now stands at 26%, up from 17% in 2009. And while the "nones" includes more than just the Unaffiliated/Post-Theological, breaking the data down indicates that the trend is towards a more than just simply secular population. The survey shows that more than 68 percent of the Unaffiliated believe in a higher power in the United States alone. This immediately excludes them from atheists and agnostics.

There's more to these numbers when you look deeper.

The percentage of Unaffiliated in the United States hovered between five and eight percent of the population from the early 1930s until 1990. Since then, this number has increased to 20 percent, with no appreciable increase in agnostics or atheists. This indicates that while people are abandoning organized religion at an increasing rate, they do not abandon their faith, just their buildings.

The reason for this trend is the increasing distance between religious dogma and the social realities "on the ground" regarding specific socio-cultural issues like gay rights, abortion, same-sex marriage, and others. Their Bronze Age scriptures rail against men who lay with men, women who are free to make their own decisions, and any nonbelievers who fail to accept their proprietary doctrines.

Despite this spiritual diaspora, atheists and agnostics are not gaining traction. This is due to the disconnect between two false choices facing the Post-Theological: the willfully ignorant solace of traditional religion or the nihilistic and elitist surety of a godless world – theism or anti-theism.

Post-Theological Faith provides a clear foundation for the next step in the evolution of religion. As it pokes very large holes in current religious options and dogma, Post-Theological belief fills the gap between the blind faith of organized religion and the New Atheists' nihilistic worldview. But today, organizations and companies like the previously cited Pew Research, Google, and Wikipedia struggle to clarify the theocratic who-is-who without a clear dogma, history, or foundational tome (Bible, Quran, Talmud, etc.) to fall back on. Lacking a clear distinction, they lump all nonbelievers under the misnomer of Unaffiliated. The media's challenge is distinguishing between those claiming to have faith in their proprietary god (christians, jews, muslims, rosicrucians, etc.) and those who do not claim any. This dilemma is obvious in the media's inability to agree on a term to place the faith and creed into a neat religious box. Wikipedia uses multiple terms, including non-religion, the "nones," and irreligion. Pew research refers to the movement with a particularly sterile term "Unaffiliated," and many refer to themselves as "spiritual but not religious."

This lack of clarity results in pigeon-holing the Post-Theological into groups that sometimes have wildly differing beliefs. The Unaffiliated are dumped into the same category as atheists (which they are definitely not) and agnostic (which most would find abhorrent), or some other broad category. Wikipedia confuses the issue by describing the population as part of the anti-theism movement, which they are not. Confusing the matter further, the Post-are accused of being Deists, (of which the Found Fathers of the US ascribed to), apatheists (don't care about the question), and antireligious.

This misnomer confusion leaves those who believe in a god but are unaffiliated with any church with no theological "home" to reside making the emergence of an alternative to faith or no-faith timely, given the two camps' arguments. Atheists hate the idea of god while the religious shudder at the thought of a world without one. The dichotomy between the two leaves the masses confused and spiritually homeless, searching for meaning and purpose.

There has to be a better way, and there is. The term "Post-Theological" gives a name and a place for the Unaffiliated to express their faith in a world without dogma. A unique but rapidly growing middle ground where we share the gift of faith with the religious but like atheists, without all that dogma.

Post-Theological faith is the unshakeable belief in a unifying extra-universal spirituality or force that is the source of all; call it god if you must. This foundational creed can be neither proven nor disproven using "evidence" posited by any religion, scientific analysis, person, group, or especially a preacher. This faith is not based upon divine intervention, the acceptance of the Holy Spirit into your soul, or some foundational tome like the Bible, Qur'an, or Torah.

Being Post-Theological is a choice made by informed humans independent of "divine" encouragement or demand. The Post-Theological god, does not have a personal interest in humans, let alone a single human.

Critical to Post-Theological faith is the understanding that this cosmic force is extra-universal, which means that it exists outside of our observable, quantifiable universe and, therefore, beyond human ability to comprehend. This makes any attempt to describe or define it useless – even to argue whether it exists or not is pointless, let alone think that we can know which day of the week it wants us to go to church.

People who define themselves as Post-Theological have a clear and powerful belief that something is at the cosmic controls while at the same time realizing it is impossible to posit who, what, how, or why. Being Post-Theological does not mean being antireligion or anti-theist. Post-Theological individuals have an inherent respect for other religions (up to a point). Unlike atheists, the Post-Theological understand that faith is a very necessary and very human trait. They accept that religion is a result of human fear, insecurity, and love but can be tyrannical and abusive. From an ideological perspective, the Post-Theological reject atheism's lack of compassion for human fragility and the shitty existence, so many people experience on the planet.

And because a Post-Theological person has no attachments to the dogmatic rules each religion uses to try to implement "god's will," the idea of either attacking or rewarding another person because of his or her beliefs is alien. Religious based conflict like the barbarity of ISIS and the Saudis' misogyny make little sense to the us, the Post-Theological. We see it as we should, cruel and stupid.

This detachment from religious affiliation is not the same as uncaring or lacking compassion. A truly Post-Theological person understands the fragility of life and the incredibly fortunate circumstances that allowed humanity to emerge from the primordial ooze. It is the closest thing to a miracle we can ever hope to experience.

I contend there are many more Post-Theological than the numbers indicate; that many christians, muslims, and jews fall into the population without knowing it. The "cafeteria" approaches many followers take to their religion means a large number of those who consider themselves members are excluded by those who make the rules. Not consciously Post-Theological, these semi-enlightened masses are pushed from their faiths into that category because their beliefs or refusal to believe certain religious dogma violate their own religions' exclusionary clauses. If you take the time to compare your everyday beliefs and actions with those mandated by your religion, you may find that you are Post-Theological by default.

All monotheisms have a number of deal-breakers that can unknowingly trigger a member's exclusion. Your sexual preferences, the compassion you have for "pagans," and even use of alcoholic beverages can exclude you from the "faithful." If you believe that, contrary to the rules of your religion, if you are a good person and live a good life, you will still go to heaven, according to those who make the rules, you are mistaken. If, as a muslim, you choose to believe that a person who rejects islam is not doomed to eternal damnation and therefore it is not your duty to find and kill them, don't bother visiting your mosque this Friday. If, as a catholic, you feel you have a right to receive Communion even if you are living with a partner out of wedlock, according to the tenets of your church, you are committing a mortal sin and will be damned to hell forever. If you are a liberal catholic and believe a jew who lives a good life will go to heaven, then whether you like it or not, the catholic hierarchy no longer considers you one of them. If you are a muslim who believes homosexuality is not a crime, you are out. If you are a jew but feel that other religions, especially islam, have a pathway to everlasting life, your rabbi wants to have a word with you.

Christopher Hitchens said it best: "If you are going to claim your religion gives you the authority to condemn people because they are homosexual, then by what authority can you claim that as a member of that faith you do not condemn homosexuality." He is correct to point out this all-too-apparent flaw in the logic of cafeteria catholics or any other faith.

Because dogma is both the corrupting and immutable characteristic of all major theisms, we as the Post-Theological reject it. We reject that these self-serving rules can ever be a means of creating a just and humane society. Ultimately, the human psyche will use the proprietary interpretation of "my god, not yours" to control and manipulate the masses who come to believe in them.

Being Post-Theological means having the underlying belief that we can never know, define, describe, or understand god.

That frees us to create a kind and egalitarian world. Knowing that humans are without the facilities to conceptualize anything extra-universal frees the Post-Theological from the need or ability to create dogma. The absence of a defining Testament or historical written word leaves the Post-Theological with no self-righteous authority to tell others how to live our lives.

The Post-Theological live purposeful lives governed by secularist, humanist, and egalitarian principles.

2

FAITH ISN'T BAD; DOGMA IS BAD

"Dogma is a principle or set of principles laid down by an authority as incontrovertibly true."
Wikipedia

Let's begin with the premise that faith in a supreme force or being is not in and of itself a problem. Beliefs are benign as long as they stay beliefs. People believe in many things that cause no harm, ghosts, fairies, leprechauns, etc.

But because all religious dogma's purpose is to define my god's words and intentions – not yours – it will always cause conflict. All dogma is inherently divisive and culturally biased.

Whether you believe it or not, the factor most predictive of the religion you, the reader, embrace is geography. The place you live as you read this page predicts your foundational religious beliefs more than any other factor; it isn't predicted by any epiphany you've had, not by any scripture you've read, and certainly not god speaking to you and coming into your heart.

It comes down to which continent, country, family and perhaps even the neighborhood you chanced to be born in. That is an indisputable fact, regardless of what you think. Every religion has an overarching geographical anchor based on its past and political, social, and migration/settling history. Ask yourself how many people you grew up with believed something theologically different? Look at the political institutions, the local school systems, the local churches/synagogue/ temples, and how they influence and reinforce the dominant religious creed.

This means that human interpretation of divine intent cannot escape the cultural, historical, societal, and geographical forces acting on the interpreter; all religion is local. (Egyptians believed that sodomy caused earthquakes. Pat Robertson believed sodomy caused 9/11.) This makes the writings of these so-called interpreters of god's words biased by the myths, mores, history, and culture of their geography. It is inescapable and it is divisive.

Dogma divides because no one can agree whose dogma is "true." One religion can't accept another's as doing so would cause that religion to cease to exist – a theological mail-merge. The only way dogma could cease to be divisive is if somehow everyone in the world could agree on the same dogma. Now that would be a miracle!

And since all dogma is a local human interpretation of religious scripture, it is impossible to engage in a discussion/debate that might change the other side's perspective. After all, if my god said it, it must be "incontrovertibly true." Contemporary islam forbids the interpretation or discussion of the Qur'an by anyone, including mullahs or other islamic clergies. Other monotheisms try to confine interpretation to the clergy of their respective faiths. The inability to intelligently discuss and criticize dogma makes it inflexible and authoritarian. Without free discourse and discussion, religions resist change and an evolving mindset.

In dogma's defense, religious thinkers make the counterargument that religion has evolved over the centuries... and it has, but not as the result of open debate and discussion. Religious evolution came from the realization by the reluctant theological hierarchy that without these changes, they faced irrelevancy. The glacial pace of modernization by major religions is a response to the fear of losing their sheep, the emptying of their pews, and the attrition of their major financial patrons. If they had their way, we would still be burning people at the stake and believing that the sun revolved around the earth – you know, the good old days!

Ultimately, dogma is a human creation serving only its creators' purposes; it does not serve god/the Unknowable. Specific dogmatic rules and commandments may differ from religion to religion, but their purposes do not. These highly questionable words of god are anthropomorphic, self-reinforcing principles based upon the need for security, purpose, power, or some other earthly desire. Dogma is a set of self-serving theological rules created by men (well, mostly men) to control the masses, sometimes to good ends and sometimes to bad.

One illustrative example of self-serving dogma is the catholic celibacy rule. Most christians equate the (questionable) fact that Christ never married with the idea that the purity of celibacy creates a stronger, holier person. They believe that celibacy makes a priest purer (There are many places we could go with that... but we won't). The reality is that the church instituted celibacy in the Middle Ages to protect church property.

At the time, the catholic church was losing its wealth to the rightful claims of the families of dead or dying priests. It realized the only way to protect itself from handing over its riches to those legally entitled was to forbid priests from entering into marriage contracts. Dogma at its most cynical. Islamic dogma proclaims that a man is worth two women. This teaching is not just a basis for sexual repression and violence; it is a foundation of Islamic law in which two women's testimonies are needed to counter that of one man. In a male-dominated society, this helps keep those in power in power.

Dogma is about knowing – knowing that our god is the only god that matters. But we take it further. We not only know that our god is the one true god, but we know him so well that he tells us what he wants. He tells us which day of the week to keep holy, he tells us to abstain from sex before marriage, he tells us to avoid the use of birth control, he tells us what actions and activities are sinful and he tells us how to deal with unbelievers. Dogma begets dogma, which begets more dogma, ad infinitum, ad nauseum, and blah, blah, blah... I kill you.

Through the age's preachers and prophets have given the world their interpretation of god's word in the Bible, Qur'an, Talmud, etc. Each swears their particular manifesto contains the words dictated directly by their god.

Joseph Smith, the illiterate founder of mormonism and convicted imposter, made his wife sit behind a blanket in their kitchen as he "dictated" the words of god to her because he'd lost the golden plates given to him by the angel Mormoni. His first wife, Emma, was the initial scribe assisted by their neighbor, Marin Harris. Mr. Harris's wife, having been quite put off by her husband mortgaging their farm to help Smith, stole more than fifteen hundred pages of the dictated text challenging the self-proclaimed Prophet to reproduce them if he was so divinely inspired. Smith could not, insisting the angel had conveniently provided a newer and better set of inscribed plates. And today, the mormon (for some reason, suspiciously close to the word moron) church has more than 14.8 million members across the globe. Go figure.

Every religion has a story like the yarn created by Joseph Smith, someone claiming that god, or an angel, burning bush, or some other imaginary event happened in which god spoke directly to them. And these divine words not to be questioned even though the timelines and machinations cannot be justified by rational logic or proven by multiple eyewitnesses because they are, well... divine. Give me a break.

Side note: Whatever happened to miracles? In the early days of christianity you couldn't step outside your house without someone curing you of something. Today, we swiftly debunk supposed miracles as natural or staged phenomena.

In the end, it is an act of human arrogance to believe we can know what the Unknowable wants from us. The idea that any of us can have enough moral certainty to know we belong to the one true religion is ludicrous, arrogant, and divisive. Just the idea of a "one, true religion" runs against secular, humanist, and egalitarian principles. But despite this, many believe that out of the thousands of gods in the thousands of religions that have come and gone on our blue planet, their god is the only true god. Sorry, but that is just stupid.

Faith is not the problem. But when belief is extended by human arrogance as "interpretation" of the divine will to the point that we believe we can intuit our personal god's desires, it corrupts human morality and dignity. Once the stake in the ground of "moral certainty" is placed, there can be no other interpretation. Religious dogma and teaching are what corrupts the world, not faith.

But it doesn't have to continue that way.

Faith would not be divisive if we all believed in our god without taking the next step to infer his or her intentions – if we just left that part out. But the temptation to create dogma and proclaim it as the only true way to know god is difficult to ignore. The Post-Theological believe anyone can worship, pray to, and give thanks to a supreme being or force. We just can't expect, intuit or complain about that which we receive or don't receive. And we do not and cannot know what this "creator" wants from us. He/she/it is not concerned with our infinitesimally small corner of the universe and most certainly does not pay attention to our actions when we are naked.

Can we believe in a god without taking it any further?

If we can, the only way to do that is to become comfortable with not knowing.

3

GOD IS UNKNOWABLE

"We don't know who discovered water,
but we are sure it wasn't fish."
Unknown

Post-Theological faith is the unshakeable belief in a unifying extra-universal spirituality or force that is the source of all; call it god if you must. The Unknowable is extra-universal, which. by definition means outside human ability to understand, conceptualize, or ideate. When we attempt this, our conclusions will always be wrong. Like describing color to a blind man, describing an extra-universal anything is impossible. Lao Tzu said it best, "The Tao that can be told is not the eternal Tao. The name that can be named is not the eternal name."

We live in a reality where everything is defined by its opposite – light/dark, hot/cold, love/hate, man/woman. Opposites define our world and our definitions; it is impossible to think of or describe a world in which opposites do not exist. The human mind is not capable of ideating such a world.

"We don't know who discovered water, but we are sure it wasn't fish," clarifies the dilemma of defining an extra-universal anything, let alone a supreme being. Swimming in our lives' reality makes it impossible to truly ideate something outside of our universal experience. The only words and ideas we have to describe are human words and human ideas based on all we know and learned of our universe. To ask the questions, "What would this being look like? What would this being think? What would this being do with his/her time? is ridiculous. There is no way we can ever know. Even the word *being* doesn't come close to describing the Unknowable.

To illustrate how difficult it is for us to ideate an extra-universal anything, try to imagine what came before the "Big Bang." According to the best minds in science, the universe as we know it began with an unfathomable explosion more than 13 billion years ago when all matter was squeezed into a space smaller than the period at the end of this sentence, referred to as a singularity. While the physics that led to this conclusion is far beyond me and anyone I know, wrapping your head around what "was" before the universe came into existence will never be explained by science. As science informs us, before the beginning of the universe, there was nothing, not nothing in the sense of the absence of something but rather nothing in the sense of the lack of anything. There was *nothing* as opposed to *something*; there was *nowhere* as opposed to *somewhere*; there was *notime* as opposed to *sometime*. Matter, space, and time did not exist. Our minds are not capable of ideating this *nothing*. There is no possible way to imagine, measure, or predict what came before because there was no *before*.

But because we humans need to know, living with "not knowing" is difficult and unsettling. Most of us find it much better to have "moral certainty" when uncertainty means less restful sleep. Coping and dealing with the unknown is one of the most challenging aspects of being human. This fear of not knowing is deep-seated and the foundation of the earliest religion – the attempt to understand the world from sunrises to sunsets, from stars to the planets, and from catastrophes to devastation. Believing that someone or something responsible for making the sun rise and set or for a good or bad growing season was comforting to people before science began invalidating the myths humans created to explain their world. There is comfort in having a reason for the seeming randomness and brutality of Iron Age life.

This holdover of the security of knowing is still important today to keep the existential angst of a meaningless existence at bay. But "not knowing" need not be so scary if we can be brave enough. For humans, the idea of letting go of this need for the comfort of knowing and accepting the idea that we cannot "know" takes courage, processing, and a lot of undoing of the knowledge we use to help us sleep at night. In many ways, we are a species whose job is to know, to find out, to discover. Knowing is what we do! We know!

And it is good to know.

Our ability to discover and come to know things helps us in a myriad of ways to enjoy and improve our lives. It has enabled us to design incredible machines, feed a huge and growing population, and solve incredibly daunting problems. Knowing is one reason we have so much; it makes our lives much more satisfying. But our knowing can also hold us back from thinking freely, that we know that we know.

This cognitive awareness – the fact that we know that we know – not only enables us to enjoy life, but it also gives us the ability to anticipate its end. We share with animals the automatic response to existential threats, but unlike dogs and cats, we dwell on the idea of death. Because we are the only species aware of our mortality, we can imagine the next step we might take after our life is over. And as we contemplate the meaning of life and death, we, even more, contemplate the meaning of *our* life and *our* death. This makes it potentially, but not necessarily, frightening to accept that the human race is simply the result of nature's laws, forces, and chemical reactions working with the right set of materials (carbon) with enough time (billions and billions – thanks, Carl).

To believe that we are just a fragile species hurtling through space on the third rock from one of a quadrillion suns flies in the face of thousands of years of religious thinking. To accept this ordinary-ness is to accept that we have no special purpose or destiny other than those we create. It can be infinitely more reassuring to believe that all life is being watched over by an all-powerful being even if he can at times be an angry old sot.

Being Post-Theological means becoming comfortable with the unshakeable belief in the impossibility of figuring out the universe. To be Post-Theological means accepting that the act of interpreting the unknowable is doomed to failure, that your very first thought is immediately and assuredly off track. It will never be possible for us humans to definitively know where we came from, why we are here, and where we are going.

A person who accepts this realizes there is no foundation for creating dogma. If we cannot ideate an extra-universal being, then how can we know what he/she/it wants? Where would it leave our lives if we had no tome or scripture or theological rules to direct our actions and life?

It leaves us with Faith. If we can become comfortable with not knowing, accepting that man can never understand or interpret God's thoughts, then the only option left is to believe or not believe without proof. The only alternative is unadulterated belief, faith – not faith in a supreme being or a life-hereafter or a list of dos and don'ts but faith that something beyond our comprehension is at the universal controls, a belief in an extra-universal force that we cannot ever know.

Living with unknowing leaves us with an opportunity to begin again; with the freedom to enjoy and experience the miracle that is life. It leaves us with a chance to create a secular, humanist, and kind world, free of the shame, guilt, hatred, and conflict all dogma promotes. Atheists believe that god does not exist without proof, and the religious attempt to "prove" their gods exist without actually succeeding at convincing most of us. The Post-Theological believe god does exist without proof. Post-Theological belief is without proof, without dogma, and without a foundational tome (Bible, Qur'an, Talmud, etc.) giving us god's word.

Let the celebration begin!

4

POST-THEOLOGICAL AS RELIGIOUS EVOLUTION

"Ye shall not round the corners of your heads."
Leviticus 19:27

Despite their seeming inflexibility, all religions evolve – mostly against their will. As human understanding of the universe has expanded, our religious belief systems developed an increasingly informed interpretation of spirituality. Early man worshiped the sun, moon, and stars. The Aztecs believed there were thirteen levels of heaven, and native Americans believe one's spirit returns to its natural state connected to all matter in the universe (closest to the pin).

These beliefs in the old gods may seem naïve and childish today, but in their time they inspired everything from brutal wars to human sacrifices. But key historical events left believers with no foundation to defend their naive and illogical beliefs and eliminated the justification for many religious-based evils. The changes in religious power and influence were initiated by an evolution of human thought and/or discovery of significant import to human understanding. These leaps moved religion to a more elevated, complex, and sophisticated role in people's lives while causing upheavals in their contemporary worlds' power

structures. Understanding these leaps and their impact on society and religion illustrates the importance of Post-Theological
thinking.

Let's begin with the idea of the Covenant between the jews
and yahweh. Crudely put, one of religions major evolutionary
steps was the agreement the jews "negotiated" with their god.
It was an unexpected and extraordinary breakthrough to begin
thinking that god and humans could make a deal. Before this
point in history, it would have been unthinkable for humans to
argue the terms of a contract with their god. To conceive of mere
humans bargaining with or even complaining to that god whose
very name was too sacred to be written down was arguably a new
high in the conception of our own exalted worth. But it is all there
in the Book of Job written shortly after the Babylonian Captivity.

Before this theological leap, man was at the mercy of the gods
and the men made by gods: pharaohs, kings, and caesars. Caesar
was a god; the pharaohs were gods, and kings ruled by the will of
god. Before judaism, there were "State" gods proclaimed by those
in power with forced worship and offerings. Man was subject to
god's (the ruler's) will; we had no negotiating power and did as
we were told – or else.

This New Covenant changed everything. The defining term
of this divine agreement was that if jews kept their side of the
bargain by obeying and worshiping him, yahweh would provide
them with a homeland and prosperity. Among other terms and
conditions, it also demanded that the jews worship Yahweh
"above all other gods." This agreement demanded that the god of
the jews be the only god, making it the first monotheism. And as
the first monotheism in a world of polytheisms, it was bound to
cause trouble. It set the jews off from other tribes making their
religious practices abominations, their gods idols, their priests
charlatans, and priestesses whores.

This earth-shaking idea of an agreement between humans and
their god elevated man's stature in the spiritual pecking order

destroying the power relationship between men and their earthly ruler/gods seriously threatening the powers that be. Theological scholars may argue this development was not the first step in religious evolution but can certainly be considered one of the most important leaps in theological thinking.

The next greatest jump forward and erosion of theological authority was Martin Luther's translation of the Bible from Latin into the vernacular, German in 1517. All previous versions of the Bible were in Latin, with the clergy as the only population fluent enough to read and interpret. When Luther and the Gutenberg Press provided widespread dissemination of liturgical teaching, it removed biblical interpretation from the hands of the theological authorities. Now anyone could and did read and interpret the words passed down through the ages. This layman's Bible replaced exclusive church teachings with personal interpretation and direct dialogue between god and man. From that moment forward, it was no longer necessary to have the foundational revelations of the Bible interpreted by the church's hierarchy. In short, the clergy became less necessary as a conduit of communication between god and man in both directions. As you can imagine, the idea of infallibility took a much-deserved big hit.

The next step in theology's evolution occurred on Saturday, June 22, 1633, in Rome. On that morning at the Vatican, Galileo Galilee was forced to publicly recanted his writings on planets' motion under pressure by the Roman Inquisition (Unlike the Spanish, everyone expected the Roman Inquisition.) The catholic church condemned his teachings as "heretical in theology and absurd in philosophy." His idea that earth and, therefore, man was not the center of the universe was so threatening that the church forbid it from being openly taught. It even proclaimed the act of looking through a telescope as heresy.

And although the church did silence Galileo, it could not repress the truth for much longer. In 1687 Newton's *Principia*

Mathematica was published validating Galileo's ideas and writings. And all hell broke loose – literally.

Though Newton's ideas had little scientific impact outside physics and astronomy, this new paradigm profoundly affected religion. His confirmation of Galileo's assertion significantly disrupted the worldview that had been in place for a very, very long time.

Since its beginnings, christianity was the foundation of Western civilization – philosophy, politics, science, family, and marriage. Virtually no area of Western life was untouched by its influence. But because of Newton and his discoveries that mankind did not reside at the center of the galaxy, let alone the universe, it became inevitable that secular forces would challenge the spiritual authority of the church and its rulers – which they did. Newton's discoveries set in motion the Age of Reason, initiating a time of intellectual thought based on observation of the natural world.

Before the publication of his *Principia*, the natural world was revealed to man by his creator through religion (clergy). If god wanted us to be the center of the universe, then we were the center of the universe – end of discussion. But now, who needed god when we could figure out the workings of the universe on our own? If one man's discoveries could undermine the foundation of scientific understanding, what other sacred cows were to be gored?

It is difficult to understate the impact of Newton's validation of Galileo's ideas on the world at the time. His writings launched the ideas of deism, democracy, the rise of human rights, and the beginnings of secular bodies of law. Newton and Galileo's discoveries threatened to relegate christianity and all its dogma to the realm of opinion at best or superstition at worst. It released a long, dammed orgy of knowledge that swept over the entire western world. In just a few decades, the power of kings, nobles, and the church was reduced or eliminated. Those that reined politically and religiously would never be the same.

The last leap of human theological understanding happened on Tuesday, November 29, 1859, with the publication of Darwin's *On the Origin of Species by Means of Natural Selection, or the Preservation of Favoured Races in the Struggle for Life*. It sold for fifteen shillings (about eight cents today) with six editions printed in Darwin's lifetime. His work created the science of evolutionary biology in one fell swoop.

Before Darwin, religion used the variety and abundance of flora and fauna as proof that god created the world specifically for man to enjoy, dominate, and consume. Until then, it was a deeply ingrained assumption that the world belonged to humans and that we stood above the animals and earth in dominance. For a time after the book's publication, the clergy used Darwin's theories as proof of intelligent design and further validated man's claim to earthly rule blessed by god. They argued that natural phenomena were physical proof that god has us in mind with his creations. And in the typical short-sightedness characteristics of all religions, the clergy never expected Darwin's opus to challenge the underpinnings of biblical revelation.

Ultimately, it was inevitable that Darwin's argument for evolution would be extended to human evolution. In his *Origin of Species*, Darwin deliberately skirted the question of humanity's place in evolution. But in 1871, Darwin squarely placed human beings with the other animals in his *The Descent of Man and Selection in Relation to Sex*. He backed up his argument that natural selection and biological adaptation, and not the "hand of god," was responsible for the rise of man and our species with research and scientific methods.

This did not go over well and the opposition was swift and stark. The idea of the survival of the fittest as the central process of life, making the world a bloody charnel house, was repugnant in a divinely ordered universe. The idea that man, just like animals, evolved from a lesser being was heresy. This meant that based on the church's belief that man is created in god's image, then god must also be of simian descent. By Darwinian thought and logic, god did not breathe life directly into Homo sapiens; he had to work with apes first.

With each leap of understanding, human beings came closer to realizing that the universe was not created for us and that we were, are, and forever will be a minor part of its vast area of time and space. Each of these great leaps forward empowered man to better understand and interpret his life, religion, and purpose. These historical tipping points essentially reinforced the same idea; that we could no longer claim humanity as the center of the god's attention or that we had a special relationship with the creator.

Each was a fundamental breakthrough or breakdown in mankind's relationship with god. To truly understand the impact of these discoveries/writings/acts as driving forces behind religion's evolution is to understand the deeply human need to believe we are special. Being sentient makes us different from all living and nonliving matter in the universe. (I think therefore I am. So logically, a tree doesn't think, so it isn't? Thanks, René.)

Believing we are special to our god is a powerful theological foundation. All monotheisms believe that it is possible to have a personal relationship with god; that god is interested in what we do, say, and think. We have the narcissistic notion that we are his special creation and not just a cosmic afterthought. And since we are so special to our god, we get to ask our personal divinity for the things we want; for forgiveness, for health, for love, for money, or anything else to satisfy our human cravings or protect us from our fears. This helps us cope with our existential angst and fear of the unknown.

But if you ponder this for a while, it may strike you as odd that we cling to this belief in our extraordinariness despite overwhelming evidence to the contrary. Since the cosmological material that makes up our DNA was blown out from our sun, the universe has regularly delivered devastating catastrophes to our fragile world. Yet despite the high level of random violence that is part of our terrestrial natural world (earthquakes, floods, hurricanes, etc.) and the extra-terrestrial world (crushing gravity, meteors, collapsing stars, etc.), we continue to believe our divine overseer would protect us, that our special relationship with our god would always save us from harm. (Well, at least for the next fifty billion years when the lease runs out.)

It is difficult to see how the religious cling to and propagate the idea that god cares for us in a special way in light of bone cancer in children, the Holocaust, the Boxing Day Tsunami, and other catastrophes. Even in the Iron Age, great tragedies like the Antioch earthquake in 526 AD that killed 900,000 people, essentially wiping out the Turkish city's entire population, never shook the local people's faith. These tragedies even strengthened people's faith, doubling down on their sacrifices and rituals to prevent further destruction from their "all-merciful" god. It is ludicrous that people thank god profusely when an unlikely survivor of some natural or unnatural catastrophe survives against all odds and is pulled from the rubble. The belief that a "merciful" god saved this person from death for some unknown reason while allowing multiples of others to perish in horrifying violence is an affront to Post-Theological thought and reason.

On the opposite hand, the faithful somehow integrates the irrational belief that our existence is due to the beneficence of a divine being with the belief in the existence of a better and blissful afterlife – you know, just in case. All theisms have their proprietary version of heavenly ascension into a "land of goz." Whether it is a place populated with seventy-two beautiful virgins (a distinctively male, islamic paradise), a land of bright light and clouds (a distinctly romantic paradise), levels of raised consciousness (a stepladder to bliss) or a Groundhog Day (much more entertaining than most – two thumbs up!) chance to make it all right, the idea of a difficult or blissful afterlife is a trademark of all religions.

And why do all religions have their proprietary version of an afterlife as a core belief? Because life would be much worse if this all-merciful god did not provide an out to the shitty existence most of us experience on this planet. We have to believe in something that gives our lives purpose. Without our self-reinforcing belief system, our lives would be pointless, right?

Each leap in intellectual understanding of the universe exploded these myths and superstitions one by one. But if you will allow me to take this evolutionary "yellow-rubric road" a step further, the next important blow to man's cosmic self-esteem may be literally right around the corner.

At some point in the near future, there will be the discovery by the Hubble Space Telescope (HST) or some other deep space probe of another "blue planet." The incredible vastness of the universe and the number of galaxies and solar systems make it inevitable. Current exploration indicates that at least two thousand planets of the right size, shape, and make-up exist in the "habitable zone" or distance from a star such as our sun. But the idea of ever communicating with or traveling to any one of them is folly. The closest identified planet with the potential for life is more than one hundred million light-years from our solar system. By the time the light from this planet reaches us, any life will most likely have come – and gone. Remember that the light from this far, far away planet traveled for 100 million years to reach us! This means that if we want to send a message to the beings that might populate this world, it will take 100 million years to reach them. So, the idea of having a continuing conversation about life on their planet or even thinking about popping by for a visit is impossible if you take the laws of physics as absolute. (I have a friend who continues to argue that it will one day be possible for humans to travel into and out of a black hole as a method for interstellar travel. I think he is half right.)

But regardless of the logistical problems of contacting that world, imagine the impact when humans realize that not only are we not the center of god's universe, but we have competition – and they were here first. While I am sure the religious community will find a way to square this to protect their proprietary theological teachings, the scientific community will welcome this as another blow to the blind belief people put in their priests and rabbis.

One very convincing contribution to the belief that we are special is the particularly human ability to achieve extraordinary feats – which we have. Just in the last 200 years, the scientific and technological advances have been extraordinary. Keep in mind that the Industrial Revolution began less than 300 years ago, a nanosecond in religion's development. Transporting a primitive man to modern times would most likely make his brain explode. The progress has been nothing short of amazing. But it has a downside many have yet to consider.

Because our species has made incredible industrial achievements and created miraculous technologies, we believe that we can overcome any obstacle if we apply enough time, resources, and effort. The optimism that is seemingly built into human DNA wants us to believe that we can do anything. In terms of the universe, this is not true. There are many things we as a species can be proud of, but we have limits.

Ask people if they believe we will successfully build a space elevator, and as long as they have no physics background, almost all will aver the idea as humanely possible. Ask any physicist, and they will tell you the mechanical and physical obstacles are not just daunting but un-overcomable. Ask someone if we will ever colonize Mars and make it a habitable planet; most non-astrophysicists believe it is possible. As long as they are ignorant on the subject, they are convinced we can build a city on another planet. Knowing that Mars atmosphere is roughly 95 percent carbon dioxide and no water exists on the planet (Don't forget that we are 98 percent water) it is impossible to sustain life there even if we could make it all that way to its surface without mishap. As it has no atmosphere, we would be subject to deadly radiation, temperatures outside of those that might sustain human life, and immediately boil our blood. (Some logistical problems are game-enders). And the sci-fi concept of terraforming is a pipedream as the previous Mars atmosphere was lost to space because of the lack of gravity and solar wind. Any attempt to produce enough oxygen to sustain life is futile.

Man will most likely never travel farther than the edge of our solar system, and the idea of creating a technology that will propel us to distant galaxies is fantasy. Regardless of how much we want to believe that man can exceed the speed of light, it just is not possible. The laws of relativity tell us that as speed increases, so does mass, while at the same time, time slows down. The closer you get to the speed of light, the more your mass increases to infinity and the closer time comes to stopping altogether (So if you could reach the speed of light, how would you know?).

It is wonderful to dream and exciting to speculate on future technologies that might allow us this power, and it makes for entertaining science fiction. But the fact is that universal distances are too far and the natural forces too great to overcome. Man will never travel through a wormhole to other galaxies or time and man will never build a spacecraft that exceeds the speed of light; it is not physically possible. We are – and forever will be – limited to our little niche of the universe. Our home planet is the only one we will ever occupy as a species.

Some see this as pessimism, but it is not. It is realistic and perhaps sobering to admit these limitations. It can be comforting to understand that man is not the all-powerful inventor we like

to think of ourselves. To save ourselves, our planet, and our species, we must accept the fact that we are on our own in the universe. We must embrace that we have no one to thank or blame
for the value and purpose of our life but ourselves, that there is
no other planet to colonize or pollute – this is it. God does not pay
attention to our little world, so the odds of an invisible man in the
sky bailing us out of our dilemmas is not a plan B.

This idea will free some and terrify many.

5

POST-THEOLOGICAL MORALITY

"Good people will do good, and bad people will do evil.
But for good people to do evil – that takes religion."
Steve Weinberg

A key argument used by people of faith in defense of organized religion is that dogma creates a good society: that faith helps civilize our world. Christians, jews, and muslims all believe their dogmatic, religious framework provides humanity with a divinely inspired guide to right and wrong. They contend that without man's interpretation of god's word into a set of commandments, hadiths, or supreme laws, the world would be a horrific landscape of rampant crime, murder, and corruption – that without dogma, there would be no source of objective morality. This argument is highly questionable and overly dramatic.

It is fairly easy to make the opposite argument: that monotheisms are not moral but immoral.

Let's start with christianity. Christians believe that anyone who doesn't accept that a carpenter's son from the Iron Age is the son of god will burn in a horrific hell for eternity. Think about that for a moment. For the crime of being born and raised in any non-christian country and accepting the beliefs you were raised with and taught by your parents, you will, according to christians, "have flesh burned from the bones until crisp and then restored by Satan to begin the burning again." Oh, and by the way – this will go on for eternity.

To understand the immorality of this concept, think about it this way: A god who is all-powerful creates a world in which billions of people are by chance born into a culture and geography that automatically dooms them to eternal torture and pain. Through no fault of their own, men, women, and children will be condemned to excruciating eternal pain while being watched by a god who can but refuses to stop it.

So, according to the christian narrative, this all-powerful being creates a world in which nonbelievers cannot escape the horrible torment he created unless they accept Jesus Christ as their savior, even if they were never exposed to his teachings. This is a vision of a god that "either cannot or will not stop the pain, thus making him either impotent or evil" (well quoted from Christopher Hitchens). How can that be moral?

Christian apologists point to the Second Vatican Council's nuanced language in defense of the church's "exclusionary clause." Vatican II was a turning point for many in the church, celebrated by the "liberal" catholics as a breakthrough for allowing more than the ancient and unused Latin language to be part of the catholic mass but condemned by the "conservative" catholics for recognizing other religions. This "liberation" of catholics allowed for non-christians to achieve eternal life. Smile, God Loves You!*

But the Council only split the hairs of belief. Vatican II reluctantly decreed that people of other faiths might enter the kingdom of heaven if they are unaware of Jesus's teachings and are good people. But those who are aware of Jesus's teaching and reject them for another faith are not welcome in their heaven.

---

* Certain restrictions may apply

(Try the other door. It's a dry heat.) This leaves jews, muslims, hindu's and any other non-christians' SOL.

Side note: The Vatican is a spectacular example of catholicism's special place in the corruption and elitism among monotheisms. It is a beautiful abomination and perversion of the teachings of Jesus. The Vatican's history of crime, corruption, and inhumanity makes it impossible for many, including myself, to enjoy the artwork without feeling shameful. If the Vatican was the birthplace of christianity, it has become its bizarre-alternative universe. Regardless of the nudges the church makes toward a more liberal creed, it does not forgive crimes committed under religious law and dogma's guise over many centuries. As the christian church grudgingly and glacially moves into modernity, it should remember that its legacy of blood, murder, and child rape will rightly take a long time to forgive, if ever. (No Saturday night confession to take away the guilt, you bastards.)

Christianity's Bible is littered with tales of genocide, infanticide, patricide, matricide, regicide, and fratricide. After a battle, Moses rages, "Kill every male among the little ones and kill every woman who hath known a man by lying with him. But all the women that hath not known a man by lying with him keep alive for yourselves." Realize that in this quote from the Bible's Book of Numbers, Moses is advocating the wholesale slaughter of children for god's sake – for god's sake! Children! Slaughter! Oh, and by the way, keep the virgins for yourself. OMg!

In the thirteenth century, the papal legate in France ordered the massacre of twenty thousand Cathar men, women, and children for heresy, reportedly saying, "Kill them all; God will know his own." In the most christianized country on the face of the earth, Rwanda, Hutus slaughtered millions of Tutsis, and the church did nothing to stop it. In fact, priests took part in the killings. Catholic bishops and priests provided Tutsi congregation members' names to Hutu's to hunt down and slaughter, a crime the Vatican stills refuses to apologize or admit. OMg! OMg! Religious morality, my ass.

Of course, these acts are not singular to christianity. It gets worse.

If you are born a muslim and decide to reject your beliefs and commit to another set of dogma (religion), you are not only banished from heaven, but it becomes the solemn duty of every muslim on the planet to kill you. It's called apostasy. (Salman Rushdie still has a price on his head even though the mullahs say they lifted the fatwa. So that you know, the muslim faith allows for lying to infidels). Muslim dogma and doctrine call for the destruction of nonbelievers, stoning women for behaviors deemed "unethical," and creating a theocracy (caliphate).

Sharia law has a number of specific punishments for specific acts ordained by god. The accommodating god of islam decided to save time and energy by bundling punishment for the combined crimes of robbery and murder into death by stoning. Alternatively, highway robbery (sans murder) is a conveniently unbundled amputation of limbs. (allah's attention to detail is helpful.) Other allah-blessed punishments include lopping off limbs for theft and flogging with a varying number of strokes for drinking. Punishment for adulterers is death.

Under islamic law, the punishment for fornication is one hundred lashes in public and exile for one year. This is called hudud or divinely condoned punishment. It is in the Qur'an and Hadiths. And if we turn to modern liberal ideas like acceptance of homosexuality and equality for the sexes, the Qur'an and Hadith are backward, misogynistic, repressive, and downright stupid. All schools of sharia law agree that any form of homosexuality is a crime; they only disagree on the type of punishment for what is called liwat. Some argue the Hadiths demand members of the LGBT community be imprisoned while some believe homosexuality is a form of adultery and must be dealt with the same as adulterers – death.

Islam has a variety of ways to administer capital punishment. One imam recommends toppling a wall on sinners or burning them alive. Another islamic leader says the best way to deal with blasphemers, adulterers, homosexuals, or other crimes against allah is to throw them headfirst from the top of a minaret – and then stone the body. Nice guys, these imam assholes.

Muslims must follow the Qur'an with no complaints; they cannot speak against or question it and cannot think anything that does not support it. If you are a muslim, you must adhere to the rigid dogma or else. Suffice it to say that if you are anything but a straight, male, obedient Arab islamist, you're pretty much screwed in that society.

And the list of muslim immorality goes on and on and on. In India, Africa, and the Middle and Far East, the religious use their dogma to justify honor killings, child rape, sexual crimes, and murder. Religiously sanctioned genital mutilation (or hymen-reconstruction surgery, if you please) is condoned and common in many African countries. It aims to keep women pure – at least until an old pervert wants to have his way with her. And don't think that this isn't as much a muslim problem as common practice in all islamic countries, including the "moderate and secular" Turkey.

Even buddhism is not exempt from religious conflict and institutionalization of evil. Zen buddhists aided Hirohito's construction of the Japanese Army that laid waste to China, murdering thousands upon thousands of its people. The Kamikaze pilots of World War II were products of the Shinto State (shintoism is greatly influenced by zen buddhism) recruited and trained for the emperor/god Hirohito's glory. Only by propelling themselves into an enemy ship could they attain the grace of god; keep in mind that the word kamikaze translates into "divine wind." Today's Dalai Lama is clearly a champion for human rights and equality, but the fifth Dalai Lama in 1660 ordered children massacred "like eggs smashed against rocks." The Saudis enable wahhabi mullahs to preach jihad and carry out suicide bombings that kill innocent women and children – just as long as they don't do it in the kingdom.

The ancient jews slaughtered the Hivites, Canaanites, Hittites, and any other civilizations that threatened their lands and all on the orders of yahweh. And while religion is not always the foundation of conflicts like war, it is often used to justify the carnage as it did in the slaughter of millions of our heathen Native American tribes in America's shameful Manifest Destiny. Believing themselves to be the divinely ordained, the peoples who "settled" North America set out to essentially create a "new heaven" by driving the indigenous population to near extinction. It is not an understatement to refer to this as a divinely justified genocide.

Muslims kill christians, christians kill muslims, muslims kill jews, jews kill muslims, buddhists attack hindu's in India, shi'ites slaughter sunnis, Palestinians kill Israelis and Israeli's slaughter Palestinians, and catholics kill protestants in Northern Ireland. And all in the name of god. I'm not sure the Post-Theological can rack up as much carnage done in the name of my god, not yours. We would have to try very, very hard to be as immoral as any of the world religions. Religious morality is an oxymoron.

So, in light of all this religious barbarism and inhumanity, you must ask yourself, "What is the only thing that keeps the religious extremists and evangelicals from running bat-shit crazy through the streets spreading mayhem and violence? How is it that with all the religious dogma that condones and encourages rape, mutilation, and murder, we aren't all dead or curled into a ball under a table in an underground shelter waiting for the start of a modern Inquisition?

Good question.

And the answer is... wait for it.

The only – and I repeat – only defense the world has against this kind of barbarous, dogmatic, god-confirmed punishment is secular law. That's right. The thing that keeps these fanatic, evangelical, and fundamentalist christians, muslims, hindus, jews, and other sects and religions from killing us all are secular and democratic legal principles.

The catholic hierarchy facilitated child-rape for decades, even centuries, by relocating and protecting known rapists from the reach of – you guessed it: secular laws. And don't believe the church has changed its ways under Pope Francis. Cardinal Bernard Law, protector of thousands of child-raping priests, and Archbishop Wesolowski, pedophile extraordinaire from the Dominican Republic, both reside in Francis's Vatican safely protected from secular law. Catholic leaders deliberately obfuscated, stonewalled, and delayed taking responsibility for the rape of thousands of innocent, adoring, trusting, and vulnerable children until forced to face it by secular courts, the media, and victims. If not for the media and courts' diligence, anal rape by priests might still be a common practice. Keep in mind this horror was not propagated by a few bad apples. Even priests who did not participate were aware of the abuse running rampant in the sacristies behind the altars. Child rape was systemic and evil. (A young ex-priest recently told me his reason for leaving the priesthood was rampant alcoholism and sexual addiction. Really? Even after all this?)

It is worth saying again that the Post-Theological would have to be pretty horrible to out-sin the catholic church. The creation and enforcement of a body of secular laws is and has been the only civilized defense against crimes codified, taught, and encouraged by the world's religions. Without the objective, rational and humanistic principles of secular democratic institutions, we would be awash in blood and mayhem. (Thank god for Justinian and Hammurabi!) Remember that the slaughter of muslims in the Balkans was stopped – yes, stopped – by a secular nation, the United States, in the horrible Croatian and Bosnian wars. The US saved muslim hordes from death and torture at the hands of their evil brothers regardless of their religion, regardless of their dogma, and regardless of their closed society. I am not sure any muslim country would do the same for us. And even though christians proselytize against sharia practices like assassination and suicide bombings, they would do well to remember the church's legacy of murder and mayhem through the ages.

On the other hand, the atheist argument that man is a moral animal has plenty of holes. Atheists posit that man is a naturally moral creature from birth, making religious dogma unnecessary for creating a peaceful, moral society. I am not so sure about that.

Stalin and Pol Pot's atheistic regimes, while "messianic" to be sure, didn't do any favors for the idea of inherent human morality. Stalin slaughtered millions in his attempt to eliminate christianity in his fledgling nation. Pol Pot had his people smother millions with plastic bags to create an atheistic, agrarian utopia (If there were something like divine justice, it wasn't in the neighborhood when Pol Pot died peacefully in his sleep in the jungle.) Of course, the most efficient killer in history, Adolph Hitler, came very close to eradicating one of the oldest and most prolific religions in his industrial extermination of the Jews. Even though every Nazi belt buckle had the saying "Gott Mit Uns" (god is on our side) etched on it, Hitler's regime was a god-less organization. Atheists point to Pope Pius XII's support of Hitler, which was true at the beginning of the war. But the catholic clergy soured on his methods and many ended up in the ovens alongside their fellow believers.

The most recent atheist defense of human morality is much more credible. They point to the evidence of a set of informal un-codified humanistic principles already present in the Middle East before god supposedly handed the Ten Commandments to Moses.

Add to that some biological evidence pointing to the theory that in nature, cooperative groups do better than those that do not. Atheists use this evidence as a basis for the "moral ape" argument. But these studies also show that groups are even more motivated to cooperate when threatened by an outside force. The bad news is that the external threat that forces people to cooperate most effectively is conflict; war is a wonderful means of creating strong groups. World War II was started by a society with a strong bond and belief in the worse side of man, the Nazi regime, and the Third Reich. The Nazis collaborated so well they almost destroyed the world and a race.

On the flip side, it also created the largest group of collaborative nations ever assembled in the Allied Forces that came together to fight the closest thing to pure evil we have seen on this planet. You can argue that the collaboration between the Allied forces indicates the good side of humanity, but the other side of the coin makes at least as strong a counterargument.

Given modern understanding of the ancient world, it is amazing that the dogmatic differences that foment so much present-day pain and suffering are incredibly small.

Judaism, christianity, and islam are all based on the foundational texts of the Old Testament. Jews and muslims avoid pork, and both religions include the same prophets. All three major monotheisms believe in Genesis and the five books of Moses. And all three believe Jesus was a holy man and that Jerusalem is a sacred place, but for different reasons. In islam, the fundamental question dividing sunnis and shi'ites is whether a military leader, polygamist, and pedophile (Mohammed married a six-year-old girl and consummated their relationship when she was nine) left his crumbling kingdom to his cousin Ali or the commander of his Army, Abu Bakr in AD 675.

In spite of his numerous barely post-pubescent wives, Mohammed never sired a son, and his only daughter was not entitled to the throne. The schism began when the question of whether the successor would be a blood relative to Mohammed or one of his empire's leaders at the time of his death. The sunnis choose Mohammed's adviser, Abu Bakr, while the shi'ites choose

Ali, Mohammed's cousin and brother-in-law. These seemingly small and irrelevant differences between the sunnis and shi'ites continue to justify countless millions of religious murders and suicide bombings.

The differences between judaism and christianity are just as insignificant. In christianity and judaism, the question of whether an Iron Age man was the son of god or just a messenger spawned incredible hatred, antisemitism, and violence. Really? Seriously? Who cares? Jews believe Christ was a prophet and teacher sent by god, while christians believe Jesus Christ was the messiah. Jews are still waiting for their messiah; Christians already have theirs. It's just kind of a difference in timing. As for the crucifixion, christians believe Jesus had to sacrifice his life to save the world. Jews don't think all that fuss was necessary. Many jews (and atheists) think that Christ's act of vicarious redemption is an abhorrent idea that leads to a lack of accountability for human sins (Confession again). The idea that a "son" of god forgave all humanity for their sins and transgressions is viewed by many non-christians as the ultimate act of irresponsibility.

Muslims accept the jewish Bible, as do christians, and many of their rituals and traditions are based on jewish teachings and ideas. The muslim practices of avoiding pork, circumcision, and fasting during the first month of the year all come directly from judaism. Mohammed had many of the same beliefs as the local jewish population in Mecca, the town of his birth.

The modern impact of these Iron age beliefs can make it ridiculous to navigate the world we live in. I currently live in Thailand, for several business and personal reasons, I emigrated to the Gentle Kingdom a year ago. My business takes me to most of the Asian-Pacific countries every week.

You may find it interesting to know that buddhism is the official religion in Thailand practiced by more than 95 percent of the population. The Thai King (currently Rama X, who ascended the throne in 2018 lives in Germany with his 20 concubines and more than 40 billion dollars absconded from his subjects) is the head of the country's Buddhist religion. (FYI, Rama X, whose real name is Maha Vajiralongkorn Bodindradebayavarangkun, thus the much-appreciated moniker, has proven himself to be not quite half the man of his father despite his exalted position. During the recent COVID outbreak, he flew his harem and staff from Germany to Bangkok for an evening dinner while many of his people were starving and desperately poor. Sukarno, feed your people!) Many neighboring countries, including Laos, Myanmar (Burma), and Cambodia, are buddhist.

My job demands I get on a plane each week and fly to a distinctly different country and embed myself in their culture. Unlike most tourists and other western business travelers, my job requires I become intimately familiar with the local culture and practices.

Let's start with India. Beef is banned in Delhi and cows are allowed to roam unmolested through the streets. This inevitably not only mucks up rush-hour traffic (which is every hour in this seething metropolis of northern India) it allows radical hindus to savage and ethnically cleanse their neighbors. Cow vigilantism (which unbelievably to people in the west, is a thing) runs rampant in certain sections of India. And today, many perpetrators feeling empowered by the surge of Hindu Nationalism ushered in by the Modi election in 2015. Modi has a history of anti-muslim positions which some have taken this as a green light to "cull" the northern part of the country of beefeaters.

However, in nine out of twenty-nine Indian States consuming beef is common practice. In the southern state of Kerala eating beef is not only common, but one of the sayings often heard there is that "A Nasrani (district of Kerala) meal is not complete without beef fry." A beef fry is a local delicacy made with Indian spices and beef, which is very popular. There was a movement towards vegetarianism in India around 400 BC led by the jains (who will not even swallow a fly), hindus, and buddhists. Before that time, cows were ritually sacrificed for special events like weddings and important guest visits. Today, partially because the current government refuses to stop it, lynching's of muslims by hindus is a growing punishment for those suspected of eating beef. Recently, Modi even took the step of banning buffalo's slaughter, one of the only available protein alternatives to non-hindu populations.

With all this fuss around cows and their consumption, it seems logical that hindus might agree why the bovine population is so revered, but most don't. For some, cattle are revered and protected because they are believed to be the Hindu god Dev's children. For others, cows are the symbol of female docility, purity, and nourishment. Regardless of the underlying mythology (let's call it what it is), in modern India, hindus use it to justify their political and social causes to the point that murder is justified just by implying the victim snacked on a hamburger. (McDonald's has adapted by offering nothing but chicken and fish in the country, but the hindu population initiated a McBoycott in 2019 due to the announcement that McDonald food was Halal (read islam) friendly).

It gets even more ridiculous. Recently, I flew from Delhi non-stop to Jakarta. Upon my arrival in Indonesia, the airplane public address system warned all passengers to leave any pork products on the plane. Being caught with bacon bits or pork rinds will precipitate a fine and confiscation. Indonesia is majority islamic or muslim at more than 60 percent ascribing to the teachings of Mohammed. How a narrow majority can exert control over the entire country because of their fear of swine is beyond me. To deny anyone access to any protein-based food source is ridiculous in this day and age, especially when the foundation of the argument came from ancient self-serving, barely post-homo-erectus men.

The pendulum doesn't have to swing too far to encounter a completely different (and just as backward) culture. The Philippines' population is 86 percent, not just christian, but roman catholic, no less. Christians, including catholics, make up more than 92 percent of the Philippine population. Prior to the colonial incision by the Spanish in the 16th century (the country's name was bestowed upon the archipelago after King Philip II of Spain, son of the English King Charles V and Queen Isabella of Portugal, which means he wasn't even Spanish, conquered the country) the majority of the population was animistic and described by established religions as superstitious and pagan. ("Save the pagan babies!" she cried.)

The only christian nation in Asia (according to the country's website) before conversion to catholicism, Philippinos practiced the belief that there is no distinction between the spiritual and the physical realm and that sentience exists in all things, not just living things. Moving to catholicism was a step backward.

The Philippines' crisis of mental health and addiction issues is regularly dealt with as spiritual problems rather than emotional sicknesses. People here are encouraged to turn to their god and his servants for direction and solace. "Pray away" the depression is common advice, as is warning the depressed that committing suicide means you will be damned to hell for all eternity. Literally between a rock and a hard place!

As for Middle Eastern countries, both alcohol and pork are banned in all the major countries, but you can get both easily if you happen to descend from one of the royal families. Halal cuisine is the hypocrisy espoused by conservative islam even as the rich and powerful eat as much western food as they like.

In the light of modern-day society and knowledge, these differences are minimal and explainable in the cultural contexts based on texts taken from oral traditions that may or may not be indicative of the original faith's founders' teachings. And the acts perpetrated by the three monotheisms to defend their right to be right have a horrible legacy and do nothing to support their moral objectivity argument even today. On the benign side, these different creeds result in religious elitism and the pedantic condescension that runs rampant from the pulpits, temples, and mosques. On the other extreme, it sanctions murder and mayhem.

An often overlooked or accepted argument against the need for divinely inspired rules of social behavior is the method religions use to encourage their believers to live by their doctrines – coercion. According to the religious model of behavior, people aren't moral out of an inherent, altruistic, humane value system of care for fellow humans. In religion, people are moral because if they aren't, they suffer the consequences. Christianity uses the carrot of eternal bliss in a billowy paradise and the stick of eternal damnation. Judaism uses the wish for a heavenly afterlife and fear of god's wrath, while islam uses the choices between seventy-two virgins or damnation, most likely without anything even close to a virgin. Even buddhism and hinduism have their versions of a spiritual scorecard used to earn enough karma to earn a step up or down the food chain. When asked if he believed that god gave him "free will," the writer, Christopher Hitchens, Vanity Fair editor, and atheist, responded, "Have I any choice?" Good answer because according to christianity and any other religion, we don't.

The false choices of cruel punishment or desire for a better afterlife do not in any way add up to free will. We are free to choose any action we want but cruelly and eternally punished if we pick the wrong one. How does that make us free again? And in most religions, you don't even have to commit the crime to deserve punishment; you just have to think it, and you are guilty. George Orwell's idea of "thought-crime" in his book A Brave New World comes directly from the sixth commandment, "Thou shalt not covet thy neighbors' wife." (Right, but the Vatican can covet all the gold and riches it wants.) Since earliest schooling, we've all been taught that being coerced to do something is not as noble as doing things for the "right reasons." But it seems religion gets a pass from this, using blatant coercion as its most powerful tool to "keep people good."

This brings me to the one final desperate argument the religious use to defend their specific teachings and dogma when all else has been negated by reasoned argument. In a last-gasp effort to justify their crimes and convince us that the morality of religion holds a privileged place in the world, they blow the dust off their trusty, well-worn (and threadbare) argument that religious charities and institutions do many more good works than atheists – that without religion and religious dogma there would be no one to provide for the poor, sick and underserved. They argue that their religion calls people to help and minister to the impoverished peoples of the world, making them indispensable. They then point to the lack of atheist charities and institutions that regularly minister to the under trodden.

This is a ridiculously easy and simple argument to counter.

When comparing themselves to antitheists, the religious are correct to state that few international atheist charitable groups provide supplies and support for the world's poor. There have, however, been recent efforts by the atheist community to energize and mobilize these efforts, especially in Haiti after the devastating earthquake of 2010. But in relation to the size and number of religiously driven charitable organizations, atheist aid groups are dwarfed by christian, jewish and islamic aid to the poor. There is no credible argument to the contrary, and this is not the issue.

The problem is religion's intentional use of a narrow definition of charity. Religions define charity as directly tending to the poor and needy. But on a broader level, charity is the physical, economic, and medical support for people in need. This broader and more realistic definition blows a huge hole in their argument. The world's secular governments (mostly the US and European) and institutions (NGOs) of the Western world have done much more than religious organizations to support the poor, hungry, and oppressed in the world... and without a religious agenda. The US – ahem, secular government – provides more foreign and domestic aid than any religion by a huge margin. Nations in Europe, Australia, and South America, and other countries donate large amounts of money through NGOs, the UN, the Red Cross, and other organizations without asking for any commitment to a specific religious doctrine. Can we say the same for any faith-based charity? While aiding the underprovided, the only agenda promoted by these non-religious institutions is free, democratic, and secular societies. Médecins Sans Frontiers, founded in France, a particularly secular country, is a clear example of non-ideological self-less charity funded and executed by good people without thought to their patient's religious, political, or ideological beliefs. The same can be said for OXFAM and other non-denominational charity organizations.

There *are* many good people of faith bringing relief and support to underdeveloped countries and places. The relief money they provide to places devastated by earthquakes, tsunamis, and hurricanes is noble, but their totals are small compared to public and government aid and medicine.

Even Catholic Charities, which boasts of being the biggest provider of service and support to the poor in the US (never mentioning secular aid in its braggadocio), has a history of requiring a commitment to christian principles in return for aid. Encouraging the spread of AIDS and other sexually transmitted diseases by requiring forswearing contraceptive use to receive aid in backward parts of Africa is unforgivable. Mother Teresa preached against the use of contraception in the over-crowded and disease-riddled slums of the world. The catholic church has a history of forbidding the placement of foster children into homes of same-sex couples and some branches of Catholic Charities have eliminated domestic partner benefits for employees in clear violation of secular laws. So much for self-less charity.

In the United States, Medicaid, Medicare, Welfare, and the Supplemental Nutrition Assistance Program (SNAP, or Food Stamp Program) do much more to keep people out of poverty than any religious group – and they don't ask you to attend church, temple or mosque in return.

To be fair and in deference to the atheistic desire for a more peaceful world, I hope humanity is moved to goodness for our species' long-term survival. I hope we can realize that self-interest works against the common goals of our community and species. But it is far from clear whether the world will spin out of control without religious "moral governance," and historical evidence seems to show that we may need some work there still.

Post-Theological faith and secular, humanistic institutions are the best hope for our race. Strong, balanced, and independent judiciaries create moral societies that focus on today's problems instead of wishing for deliverance from a violent world into the hands of an angry god.

6

POST-THEOLOGICAL FEMINISM

"The word and works of God are quite clear, that women
were made either to be wives or prostitutes."
Martin Luther, Reformer (1483-1546)

When it comes to women's role, religious dogma runs the gamut from relatively benign chauvinism to brutal misogyny. Religiously sanctioned repressive practices like discrimination, denigration, violence, and sexual objectification are common to western and eastern. None of the world's major religions truly believe in women's equality in their preaching, writings, or practice. Every religion on the planet preaches a misogynistic doctrine stretching from restricting women's rights to permitting rape and murder. And most of it is fueled by men's fear of succumbing to the lure of female sexuality. It is ludicrous that muslim men make their women wear all-covering garb, so they don't tempt them. (Man up, and control your biological urges, you culturally retarded imbeciles!)

It's not difficult to understand how this came to be when you consider all the major theological tomes were written and interpreted by primitive men with little education or worldly experience. And at the time most were penned, male societal dominance and control was the rule; female-based governance was a rare – very rare – exception.

Let me begin with the oldest monotheism, judaism, as a religion and social/cultural phenomena. We can start in biblical times when jewish society distinctively favored men over women. According to early judaic dogma, husbands could divorce their wives but not the other way around. Women could only divorce with their husband's permission. It's gotten better since then – but only somewhat. The move toward reformed judaism is late but better than never. Modern judaism shows some attempts to become more liberal and equal. Still, Rabbi Joseph B. Soloveitchik, an important leader and thinker of the modern jewish community in the United States, prohibits women from playing any jewish leadership role. Many jewish men declare that their women have rights, but you don't see hasidic or orthodox jewish families with strong, professional matriarchs. Ultra-orthodox women are repressed second-class citizens that must submit to their husband's demands, including having sex at specific times of the day. Recently a group of hasidim "men" delayed an airline flight until they were seated a "respectable" distance from female passengers. Really? In this day and age, you cannot even sit close to women for fear of what... cooties? What are you... children? What is this... elementary school?

Christianity has long been known for its subjugation of women and fear of female power. Even in this modern age, it still has an exclusively male hierarchy – exclusively. (To their minimal credit and after years of stonewalling, protestant churches are now allowing female ministers.) The catholic papacy allows the good nuns to play an important role in charity works and keep the church clean as long as they don't become too self-important. Long-suffering nuns have carried the church's banner for centuries despite being banned from administering sacraments or performing common rituals.

One terrible but inevitable result of the nun's subservient role was their inability to expose priests' rampant pedophilia activities. Like nonparticipating priests but with less power, they kept to themselves and looked the other way. Unlike those priests, they did this out of pressure from the catholic hierarchy, not because they were protecting their own man/boy love clubs like their clergy. Christian sexual guilt, demand for subjugation, and fear of seduction attest to the church's legacy of misogyny. Tertullian, one of the church's original fathers, described a woman as "the gateway of the devil" and "a temple built over a sewer." And while liberal catholic thinkers today point to how far the church has come, they forget that the church's past crimes are not forgiven as easily as confessing its sins on a Saturday night. It seems a rigid penis makes pious men unable to accept blame for their sins.

The Church of England was founded by Henry VIII, whose reputation with "the ladies" (and the papacy) was mixed depending on whether you were on his good or bad side. His hobby of lopping off the heads of wives who could not bear him a son was second only to that of using his church to rationalize his predatory ways. Keep in mind that even today the Queen is also the head of the Church of England. The church takes little responsibility for its repression of women throughout the ages. If it did, today's clergy would admit their transgressions and make amends.

Let's expose the evangelicals for what they are while we are at it. You would think that twenty-first-century liberal thought would be so ingrained in our society that christian evangelicals would consider changing their gender bias to accommodate women's interests... but no. Evangelical churches regularly practice the "second-classing" of women sidelining them to the roles of teaching children and denying them a voice in church affairs. Evangelists cherry-pick Bible verses to subjugate the female members of their flock and keep them powerless.

Marc Driscoll, the fallen pastor of Mars Hills Church in Seattle, one of the fastest growing and fastest declining evangelical institutions in modern memory, referred to women as "penis homes," calling them "weaker vessels." He stepped over the line by using church money to buy up ten thousand copies of his terribly written book in a not-completely-thought-out trick to reach the top of the New York Times Bestseller List. He now describes himself as being in his post-angry-young-preacher period wanting to be considered a wise-Bible-elder. (I guess he doesn't consider Pride one of the Seven Deadly Sins.) As of this writing, Driscoll has resurfaced in the Arizona desert, calling himself a redeemed man worthy of leading again. And he has more than a half-million followers.

Evangelicals (and mormons) continue to place women in submissive roles while trying to appeal to younger audiences. But I find it difficult to determine why a woman would subject herself to a life of subservience and second-class citizenry. But then, most evangelical movements revolve around a persuasive and charismatic leader who usually is very good at convincing people to do things against their own best interests.

Let's pile on the buddhists, shall we?

Buddhism is more egalitarian in some respects than, let's say, the catholic church (not a high bar). Still, it reveres male monks over female while reinforcing male domination within the sect and society. It neglects to speak out against the inherent gender inequalities in Asian society and culture, and men play the main roles in temple duties. The Buddha originally refused to ordain women as nuns or monks preaching that allowing women into the temple would cause his teachings to survive only half as long – five hundred years instead of a thousand (sounds enlightened, doesn't it?). And while later teachings recognized gender as part of "samsara" or the veil that obscures the truth and so cannot define who can achieve nirvana, other teachings dictate that a woman can only achieve enlightenment after being reincarnated as a man and then dying (as if they didn't have it tough enough already).

Hinduism might be better... oh but wait! The Vedas.

Their version of the Psalms state that women are subservient to men. Despite having female deities, women have limited rights in hindu society and are expected to care for the house and home with less access to educational opportunities. This leaves them vulnerable to abuse and neglect. Gender abortion is outlawed but occurs regularly, and, in the past at least, the early death of a husband was blamed on the wife. Widows are compelled to throw themselves upon their husbands' funeral pyre in the act of self-immolation. In many hindu villages, transgressions by women are dealt with by religiously sanctioned murder or banishment.

But the winner of the most repressive, misogynistic, and medieval dogma towards women is – you guessed it – islam.

The culture of islam is a well-oiled vehicle for repressing women's rights from the requirement that women cover themselves with the smothering abaya and burqa to the rule that they may venture out of the home only when accompanied by a family member. It is repressive and medieval and most islamic nations practice gender apartheid.

In all Arab countries, women are forced to kowtow to cultural and religious mores that keep them from driving, voting, traveling, studying, and learning, leaving them dependent on men. It is a jarring experience to fly into Dubai, a city that tries too hard to portray itself as a modern, islamic metropolis and see women covered from head to toe with only their eyes visible walking behind their husbands. And even though that city with its impressive skyline, Western entertainment, and East-West fusion cuisine appears modern and very twenty-first century, its cultural mores and religious dogma regarding women are medieval (or Neanderthal, if you like) ... and that's being generous.

Recent arguments that the hijab, niqab, and burqa are part of a new movement in muslim female identity are cynical propaganda advocated by islamic men. For a Western muslim woman, in a country where she has the right to vote, drive, and attend the school of her choice, stating that her headscarf is part of who she is one thing. But for a repressed female living in a muslim country where she has no chance of anything approaching the same equality as men to be "allowed" to express her muslim identity by wearing a smothering, stifling piece of clothing is cynical and manipulative. If the men in that society want women to have the freedom to express their muslim identity, then let them do so while driving, studying, voting, and living their lives. We welcome that.

Remember that many of these muslim men live in countries in which the marrying age for girls is nine years old and whose leaders routinely marry prepubescent girls. The Yemen government recently overturned – yes, overturned! – a law requiring female children to be post-pubescent before being married off to a much older man. (We call them perverts in our country.)

Now I know in this age of multiculturalism, it is important to be tolerant of other cultures and their practices but let's call this what it is; culturally and religiously sanctioned pedophilia or child-rape, if you like. Male Islamists dismiss the calling-out of child-brides in the Middle East as judgmental and a product of western xenophobia. But it would be interesting to interview a nine-year-old girl to get her thoughts about losing her virginity to a 40-year-old man, as is common in islamic countries. When he was twenty-eight, the Ayatollah Khomeini married a ten-year-old, calling his marriage to the prepubescent girl a "divine blessing." He advised fathers, "Do your best to ensure that your daughters do not see their first blood in your house."

Muhammad's marriage to Aisha at the tender age of six (kindly he waited three years to consummate the marriage when she was nine!) was and is common in islamic countries. A man's intentions are pretty transparent when marrying a girl not yet even old enough to conceive; it's not her ovaries he is interested in.

When confronted with this historically documented and easily validated facts, muslims point to the immorality of western culture as evil to derail the argument about divinity and god's will. Talk about throwing stones from glasshouses. This from the islamic writings according to Surah 65:4, "a man must wait three months to divorce a wife who hasn't yet reached menses." If islam allows a man to *divorce* a girl who isn't old enough to have her period, it follows that islam allows a man to *marry* a girl who hasn't yet reached menses. And if the Qur'an allows marriage to prepubescent girls, then Muhammad's marriage to Aisha would in no way rule out such a practice.

This is bullshit, and enough is enough.

Tolerating cultural differences is different than speaking out against institutionalized child rape. The perverse moral relativism that allows muslims to marry prepubescent children while condemning the west for pornography and lax sexual values should be abhorrent to all people on the planet.

A *partial* list of muslim practices that subjugate and repress women include no right to vote, drive, or divorce, being blamed and punished by family members for being raped by family members (intentional duplication), honor killings, genital mutilation, veiling, sexual slavery, beatings, child marriage, polygamy, and inability to have a say in the development of the very laws that suppress them. Holy men, my ass!

The presumption, as the Qur'an says, that "men have a status above women," is pervasive in the islamic world. It has been going on since the founding of the religion. Aisha Mohammed's child-bride once told him, "You have made us equal to the dogs and the asses." The revered islamic scholar, al-Ghazali, who has been called 'the greatest muslim after Muhammad,' writes that the role of a muslim woman is to "stay at home and get on with her sewing. She should not go out often, she must not be

well-informed, nor must she be communicative with her neighbors and only visit them when absolutely necessary; she should
take care of her husband...and seek to satisfy him in everything...
Her sole worry should be her virtue...She should be clean and
ready to satisfy her husband's sexual needs at any moment." [as
quoted from Ibn Warraq]

Then there is the special case of Saudi Arabia.

This kingdom (my ass) is made by and for privileged males
with multiple wives regularly importing Western prostitutes to
satisfy their unholy desires. Sunni islam especially wahhabiism,
the dominant form in many Gulf states, allows for "temporary
marriage." This provision permits men to gain female sexual
companionship on a short-term basis. In a temporary marriage
or mut'ah, the man and woman – or more likely pervert and little
girl – sign a marriage agreement that is ordinary in every respect
except that it carries a time limit. Once signed, the agreement
disenfranchises the woman from any claims to the husband's
money, fortune, family, or assets. Islamic tradition stipulates
that a temporary marriage "should last for three nights, and if
they like to continue, they can do so. And if they want to separate, they can do so." This practice of temporary wives essentially
allows for religiously sanctioned prostitution.

So, get this: In a society where a woman can be put to death
for being unfaithful to her husband, he can have as many temporary marriages as he likes with no fear of punishment. In fact,
this practice is encouraged. WTF is wrong with these people?

Can you imagine this happening in a society with equal rights
for women? Do we have to avert our eyes when we see overt sexual repression and abuse? It is frustrating that the United States,
which is, for the most part, a country committed to equality between men and women, fights wars to free islamic populations
from suppression and cruelty (Bosnia, Afghanistan, Iraq), allowing them to return to the practice of suppressing and beating
their women. The many brave young men who fought in Iraq and

Afghanistan returned with stories about building schools dedicated to educating women only to have them routinely destroyed not by the Taliban but by the local islamic population when left unoccupied by soldiers. Insecure muslim males kill, rape, and terrorize female populations when threatened with anything smelling of female empowerment. Islam needs to confront this institutionalized, legalized, and fundamental religious inequality before it can be considered part of the modern world.

Every modern, secular, and egalitarian nation should refuse to validate countries practicing gender apartheid by relegating them to second-tier nations' status. But instead, many enable sexually repressive regimes by allowing them to participate in international events even though those regimes refuse to allow women the same rights within their countries. (Even Starbucks changed its mermaid logo to a generic non-gender icon to appease the Saudis. Cowards.)

These misogynistic and repressive nations should be denied equal status and nations should refuse to nominate them as host countries for any international event – no Olympics, no World Cup, no International Games until they allow women the same rights they have in their competing countries. How is it that Qatar, a country that practices human trafficking, where rape and female suppression is endemic and governed by sharia law, can be the host of a world sporting event like the men's 2022 World Cup? This country is a nightmare for women and all members of the LGBTI community. Qatar should be considered a pariah and excluded from any participation in this sort of cooperative global competition.

And before I make my argument for Post-Theological Feminism, I must raise the issue of religious fear and disgust with menstruation. What is it with you guys? The men of almost every religion, including Eastern ones, are afraid of being in the same room with menstruating women. Cooties? Again? Really?

In their Tractate Shabbat, orthodox judaism states that

women are "a sack full of excrement with a bleeding hole." The kabbalist arm of judaism believes that menstruation represents women's evil character and that men should have no contact with a menstruating female. Islam forbids sleeping in the same bed; early catholicism and christianity taught the avoidance and shunning of menstruating females.

A Yemeni cleric recently explained in a television broadcast what makes women inferior and unable to serve as good witnesses: "Women are subject to menstruation when their endurance and mental capacity for concentration are diminished." Why does a natural, biological function necessary to continue our species make such cowards out of the leaders of our churches, synagogues, temples, and mosques?

Because Post-Theological belief cannot ideate a being with sexual and genital differences, it is absurd to repress women based on the "word of god." With the inability to ideate an extra-universal anything, it is impossible to assign it any gender-specific genitalia. Any extra-terrestrial force or being is beyond opposites, and with gender being one of the most divisive characteristics in religion, thank god for that! The tao-ist term "tao" may be the most useful way to refer to this force, god, being... whatever. The "tao" has no gender and cannot be described as a man or woman. "The tao that is spoken is not the true tao."

For the life of me, I don't know how women put up with it. I cannot understand in this day and age how these medieval superstitions and fears persist in all religions, western and eastern. Thank god for secular nations and laws granting and protecting women's rights. With these kinds of shallow, insecure men running major religions, I don't trust any of them to engage women in solving our deep problems. And god knows we need all the help we can get.

Studies overwhelmingly show that the single most important

factor that can help pull populations out of poverty is female education and empowerment. It is an oft-proven fact that when women have access to education, the GNP and output of a country quickly improve. Once women escape a culture of Neanderthal, male-dominated control, their health and finances improve as well. These repressive social beliefs and practices keep women and children in poverty and poor health in many, many of the world's major and minor countries in the name of religion. Simply allowing women's reproductive health options can change the balance in the battle against AIDS, STDS, and other scourges.

I am not hopeful at this point in history that it is possible to de-tach misogynistic dogma from the foundational texts on which they are based. The debilitating factor limiting religions' ability to allow women equal access and rights is that god is depicted in most religious texts as a male being. Just as the Western world depicts Christ with Anglo-Saxon features even though he was a Palestinian jew, religious texts project a god as a testosterone-ed, virile, and masculine figure. When your maker is the opposite sex, it's tough to argue for a better seat on the bus. It doesn't give women much of a chance. Islamic leaders now state that the Qur'an cannot be altered in any way, so the words relegat-ing women to the status of secondhand citizens and male pos-sessions eliminate the discussion. The roman catholic church's hierarchy is so thoroughly male-dominated and sclerotic that the odds of it ever liberalizing to the point of equal status for women is very low. As for jews, the current trend towards orthodoxy doesn't leave much hope for educated, talented, and strong jew-ish women to become part of the leadership structure with any real power. Strong women threaten the religious male establish-ments so much they feel the need to create and use words that dis-empower women and sabotage their efforts. (Femme-nazis... Really Rush? I'd love to make your Internet Search History pub-lic knowledge.)

The Post-Theological movement carries none of the Iron Age baggage and archaic dogma created by men to define women's roles to satisfy their insecurities, sexual desires, and fear of cooking. As a movement and a realization that is dawning in the modern age, we would hope it avoids the male insecurities that drive female repression and subjugation. Post-Theological belief is incompatible with current religious thought and dogma and will continue to be until these religions liberalize their belief systems to eradicate misogyny and provide equal representation by women in their law-making, dogmatic machines – if that is even possible.

Post-Theological thought supports and defends secular and egalitarian legal systems protecting the rights of all sexes. And while every couple – same-sex or other – can consciously choose traditional gender roles if they want, their rights are protected by the judiciary and the mores of a liberal modern society if they don't. If anything can help bring more equality into the world, perhaps it is a Post-Theological mindset.

For the love of god, I hope so.

7

POST-THEOLOGICAL AND ATHEISM

> "Organized religion is a sham and a crutch
> for weak-minded people...."
> Jesse Ventura ex-Governor,
> atheist and fake wrestler

So, my discussion with a, to quote him, "confirmed atheist" (funny to use a term usually associated with catholicism to defend your non-faith) allowed me to explain that his underlying assumptions are identical and somewhat more inflexible than believers.

"So, you are a confirmed atheist? I asked.

"Yes, I am."

"Then, you believe there is no god. Am I correct?"

"It isn't a belief. I just know it."

"Well, then how do you *know* it?"

"I know it because there is proof that god doesn't exist."

"Oh, really, like what?"

"Like the fact that there is so much evil in the world." He replied.

"Okay, but then to what do you attribute all the good in the world?"

"There is much more evil than good in the world." he retorted.

"Well, we might be able to argue that point, but regardless of which is more, and which is less, how does the existence of evil prove that there is no god?"

"Because a god would not allow such terrible things to be done in his name."

"So, you are attributing a human characteristic, compassion, to a non-human entity." I challenged.

"With all the evil deeds men do, there is no way we could have been created in his name."

"You seem to know quite a bit about this god who doesn't exist."

"Well, I guess you think god made the world and the universe?"

"I don't know. Because god is impossible to know, how can I even begin to think that I know what he does or doesn't do?"

"My point exactly." He said confidently.

"Actually, it is the opposite of your point. You said that if a god existed, he would be compassionate and create a world that was good. How can you know any of that?"

"Look, if god didn't create the world, then who did?" He asked with growing frustration.

"I have no idea. It would be arrogant of me to believe that I could fathom how and why the universe came to exist and especially who or what created it."

"So, what does that leave you with?"

"Faith," I said.

"Faith in what?"

"Faith in god."

"How can you believe in something you have no proof of?"

"How can you? Look, I get that it is easier to assume you have the answers, whether it is the belief in god or non-belief in god. It is comforting to believe you are right. But a Post-Theological viewpoint is the decision to believe in a god without proof. Just as you believe in no-god without proof."

Atheists know there is no god.

They know that if there were a god, the world would be a different and happier place. They know that if there were a god, he or she would have created a world free of violence, evil, and mayhem. They seem to know quite a lot about their no-god.

There are several YouTube video-debates between christians, and atheists trying to "prove" and "disprove" each other's beliefs, without any real proof on either side. One such forum even allowed audience members to vote for the side with the most convincing argument. (Vote for me and win everlasting ... oh, wait.) But rather than using reasoned argument to convince us of the non-existence of god, many atheists use the gaps, inconsistencies, and flaws in christian, muslim, and jewish thinking and scripture to support their argument of the non-existence of an extra-universal force or being. Their primary argument seems to be that the fact that the words of the Bible, the Qur'an, and Talmud are flawed proves there is no god. Many well-known New Atheists argue that religion is evil, proving there is no god. How the existence of evil proves there is no god, I have no idea.

The New Atheists are as much convinced about god's non-existence as their opposite side is convinced of the opposite. I don't think these discussions and arguments bring us closer to understanding each other. The "fundamentalist atheism" espoused by people like Sam Harris, Christopher Hitchens, and Richard Dawkins has as dogmatic and elitist a tone as the most theological rants at times. (Sam Harris would like the world to use the word "anti-theist" instead of atheist because of the movements growing bad reputation. Anti-vaxxers want the same thing. They would like to be referred to as "vaccine risk-aware." Always best to deal with unpopular reputations by "tweaking" the brand.).

The main positive difference is that atheism lacks any formal dogma, although the New Atheists seem to want to change that. For all its ranting against religion, atheism doesn't have the history and written testament that is the foundation for theological dogma and divisiveness. Without a foundational tome like a Bible or Qur'an, there is no anchor for moral certitude or need for one. After all, no godhead leaves no head of god to interpret and exploit. Without the foundational "moral certainty" present in other religions, there is no reason to defend or promote specific atheistic non-beliefs. And their point that atheistic leaders like Stalin or Pol Pot, while messianic and cruel, used faith as an excuse for political domination and governmental takeover is valid. I doubt we need fear that an organized group of atheists is about to create a standing army to enforce their non-faith beliefs (cue the Bizarro-Crusades).

Atheists' problem is that they take it too far. Disbelief as an "ism," develops a self-righteous elitism or moral certainty about others' beliefs. Most of us, the Unaffiliated, are turned off by their condescending and pedantic nature. Christopher Hitchens led a witch hunt against Mother Teresa as a hypocrite and evil person, calling her "Hell's Angel." Really? Could you find anyone more revered by the world to attack?

The idea of "one true faith" is often integrated into atheistic rhetoric, much like those of the world's religion. Atheist dogma proclaims that there is no god. But really, how do they know this? How can they be sure that before the Big Bang, there was no Big Brother? How can they preach that all creation in the universe results from pure chance and cosmic forces? Do they really know this?

They have as little proof for the non-existence of god as believers have for the opposite. But they spend so much time trying to convince us of their non-faith that it gets annoying. Lawrence Krauss's latest book, *The Universe from Nothing* is a wonderful explanation of how our universe could have come into existence without a creator and a brilliant explanation of cosmological phenomena. But the book's main purpose seems to be refuting claims to the existence of god. Krauss's ultimate conclusion is that if the universe could occur without a god, then it did. He spends a great amount of energy and research disproving something that cannot be disproven. I am pretty sure he is preaching to his choir.

Ridiculing and debasing believers is almost an atheistic sport and not in the best interests of their movement. Stating that people who believe in god are weak is as arrogant and divisive as any theocentric statement and shows a basic lack of empathy for other human beings. Post-Theological thought proposes that it is possible (but not probable) that any religion could be the one valid interpretation of god's will. The Post-Theological respect other religions as long as they do no harm.

However, we Post-Theological believe religion gives people much-needed solace and comfort in times of sorrow and loss and is a wonderful aspect of religion. Moderate, ecumenical, and inclusive religions are not as evil as the atheistic cognoscenti proclaim. They are a natural and perhaps stodgy creation to help man deal with the dilemma of being human. Astronomer Carl Sagan once said, "You cannot convince a believer of anything; for their belief is not based on evidence. It is based on a deep-seated need to believe." He saw faith in a supreme being as human weakness and fragility. To that, I say, exactly.

We are a fragile species on a blue planet in a cold and unforgiving universe. It is human to want to believe in something more. Losing a loved one creates a deep sense of loss and emotional pain. Wanting to believe that there is a chance of being reunited in a glorious afterlife is not a weakness. It is an emotional gift we have as sentient, caring beings.

We are emotional creatures with the gift of establishing close and fulfilling attachments to good and wonderful members of our same species. Of course, we can establish sick and unhealthy attachments as well, but you get my point. Atheists reject the idea that religion has had or can have a beneficial effect on our societies. They unflinchingly argue that religion does more harm than good and is evil.

Hitchens's most popular book *God Is Not Great, How Religion Poisons Everything*, is a cynical and negative screed that religion has brought nothing but pain to the world. He lays out the argument that when religion is placed on the historical scale of right and wrong, good and evil, there is no balance. The evil done by religion more than outweighs any positive impact and precludes any argument that might allow for the positive influence of religion or its leaders. His argument is as unbalanced as his conclusions. The New Atheists' proposition that all religion is bad intentionally ignores history and projects elitist judgment and pedantic abasement onto good and caring people. The concept of dogma makes the debate of whether religion is responsible for more good than evil or the opposite in the world pointless.

Dogma has been and is still used to justify evil, good, war, education, compassion, and hatred, whether it is muslim, jewish, or christian, or any other interpretation of god's word. It is impossible to determine whether atheism would do a better job of creating a useful society as there is no positive example in history to draw from. But there are many examples of atheistic rulers creating terrible societies. Atheists too often and too easily dismiss the positive impact of christian, muslim, and jewish values and good people's works by pointing to the evils imposed on the world by religious organizations. But their judgment invalidates the many aspects of dogma that provide for justice and good in the world. They demonize (sic) all beliefs regardless of creed or contributions. They ignore that muslims have Zakat, one of the Five Pillars of islam that preaches compulsory giving to charity and regularly give more than all other faiths in support of cancer research, relief organizations, and the needy. They dismiss or ignore facts like that the buddhist country of Myanmar/Burma contributes more to charities than the United States and almost all other Western nations on a per capita basis or that Catholic Charities funnels money to needy people in the Philippines, Africa, and Asia.

I am not sure the starving people in third world countries would agree with atheists about charity and helping the less fortunate. To dismiss the contribution of religious thought, deeds, and art to the world is naïve and self-serving. Christianity brought us Johann Sebastian Bach, Sir Isaac Newton, and Stephen Colbert. Islam gave us calculus, the calendar, algebra, optics, and Mesut Ozil. Judaism is responsible for the beginnings of childhood education, the law of thermodynamics, the understanding of infectious disease, and Jerry Seinfeld.

Religion has been the foundation of social conscience, compassion, and charity for a very long time – all religions. The christian church feeds the world's poor and sick in places few others would go. It also provided the world with the foundational structure of government, the idea of representative democracy, and incredibly beautiful buildings.

And while dogma is the divisive force in religion, there is much religious dogma promoting collaboration and cooperation. Think about the sayings, "Love thy neighbor as thyself" and "Do unto others as you would have them do unto you." Jesus, Muhammad, Vishnu, and the Buddha all preached good works and loving your fellow man.

To be fair, there is much good to be said for atheist activism and its continuing fight for separation of church and state. Early European governments came to see secularism as a necessary and beneficial characteristic of government. Like atheists, they realized that keeping religion out of government makes for a more inclusive democracy by reducing conflict and increasing the potential for common ground. Secular governments are more likely to reach broader and more pragmatic agreements.

We sometimes forget that secular, humanistic values were and are important to the creation of egalitarian forms of government and equal rights. We should be grateful for atheists' continuing struggle against governmental or cultural christianization, especially in our country. We can continue to count on atheists are one of the few groups that fight for the separation of church and state. Does anyone think that given a chance, the Constitution-loving christian Right would hesitate to amend it to define the United States as a christian country?

On the other hand, atheists would do well to remember that religious beliefs helped shape this country's values and mores. While we in the west believe theocracy as a form of government ultimately fails, we still owe much of our freedom and opportunity to religious principles. Christian values helped fashion our egalitarian and democratic government, and through it, the shared value of secular government helps ensure acceptance of all faiths.

But to be fairer, there are the many myths and untruths proclaimed by those who would have us believe that faith played a larger role in establishing the foundations of our secular US government. Our nation's founding fathers were not christians, as many, especially the evangelical, would have you believe. They were deists who did not believe in the Bible or any other man-made/written interpretation of celestial desires. Deists believe that the universe has a creator, but this creator does not meddle in humans' day-to-day affairs and does not communicate directly with humans through revelation or religious scripture.

While none of the founders were atheists believing there is a god, their use of the term god did not mean the same as those who believe in the god of the Bible. They believed Jesus was a real person but denied his divinity. We'll never know for sure, but by reading their writings, it seems that most were opposed to the Bible and the teachings of christianity in particular.

No wonder they felt the urgent need to separate church and state when you consider the divisions and violence christianity was responsible for in the countries they fled. At the time of America's founding, catholics and protestants were killing each other off in England and on the Continent by droves. Catholics were killing protestants, hugenots, and the mennonites in Holland while jesuits were being disemboweled in England by protestants. So inhumane was the mayhem that one piece of British art from the time shows "a priest whose genitalia were cut off and grilled. Forced to eat his roasted private parts, the priest was then dissected by his torturers so they can observe him digesting his meal."

When human frailty, greed, and fear become the driving force behind religion, things quickly get off track. The evil that religions do – jihad, sexual abuse, wars, and genocide – comes from the elitism and divisiveness promoted by monotheism: that there is only one god, and he is my god. This makes each religions' so-called moral certainty moral falsity. Moral certainty has forgiven many, many crimes only to be later unmasked as an incomplete understanding of the universal forces working on mankind.

And while atheism's appeal has lessened in recent years, it is understandable that the spiritual nomads look to it as one possible refuge from all religious foundational books' dogmatic teachings. Without a god, there is no godhead to interpret, so less dogma. But atheism and especially militant atheism do not offer the Post-Theological any place to hang their hat. Lumping the Post-Theological in with the atheists or anti-theists does no justice for the strong belief in a greater force we-can-never-know.

Atheism and its pedantic nihilistic elitism are contrary to Post-Theological belief and provides no home for those seeking solace and human connection.

8

POST-THEOLOGICAL
AND AGNOSTICISM

"Isn't an agnostic just an atheist without balls?"
Stephen Colbert

Agnosticism has a healthy skepticism about religion. Its core principle is that the existence or non-existence of god cannot be known. According to Thomas Huxley, who first coined the word, "Agnosticism, in fact, is not a creed but rather a method the essence of which lies in the rigorous application of a single principle ...Positively the principle may be expressed: in matters of the intellect, follow your reason as far as it will take you without regard to any other consideration. And negatively: In matters of the intellect, do not pretend that conclusions are certain which are not demonstrated or demonstrable."

Agnostic belief is comforting and non-confrontational. After all, who is going to argue with uncertainty? Agnostics refuse to play the game of who's right or wrong when it comes to the supreme being. They don't quite rise to the level of anti-theism or atheism in that they will also consider the possibility that there is a god; they don't know one way or the other. Upon initial glance, agnosticism seems to share the belief in the inability to know god and that ideating a supreme being is impossible and therefore pointless with Post-Theological thought. But it fails to take a side on the question of whether there is or isn't something or someone at the cosmic controls; it leaves the question hanging.

Agnosticism seems pointless. It is not a point of view; it is a point without a view. The idea of faith is you believe, or you don't; faith is not about knowing, it's about believing. The fact that you don't know has nothing to do with it. Atheists don't know either, but at least they take a stand. It seems that, in essence, agnostics are atheists but want to be more even-handed. It really doesn't bring anything to the party. Not having a belief one way or another doesn't leave much purpose in one's life. The idea of not knowing if there is a god creates a void that people need to fill. In his book *The God Delusion*, Richard Dawkins points out that agnostic belief has no disciplined thought process or methodology. His statement "I am an agnostic to the extent that I am agnostic about fairies at the bottom of the garden" shows his contempt for the lack of intellectual discipline behind agnostic arguments. (Richard Dawkins argues that all religious people are much closer to being atheists than they think. They need only reject the teachings of one other religion.)

Ask an agnostic whether he or she believes in god, and their answer is, "I don't know." Well, of course, they don't know. Nobody knows if there is or isn't a god, but that wasn't the question. The questioner isn't asking whether or not this person "knows" there is a god; they are asking whether or not the agnostic "believes" there is a god. The search is not for the surety of the knowledge but rather the depth of a belief. So even from a semantic point of view, agnostics avoid the question.

Many agnostics fall more readily into the Post-Theological set of beliefs than any quasi-religious limbo-land. This may be due to the lack of a spiritual home provided by theism or anti-theism and agnosticism is a convenient default used to avoid being pigeon-holed into either side of the argument. But if that is the case, then it is intellectually dishonest. Maybe the term apatheism, which is the desire to be left out of the argument regarding religion, would be a better term. Then the response to the question of whether or not you believe in a god would be, "I don't care either way."

Anyway, clearly different from agnostic beliefs or whatever they call them, the Post-Theological creed posits that the inability to know or understand god is immaterial. There is a god, but anything more than that creates troublesome dogma. The same question posed to the agnostic would be answered straightforwardly by the Post-Theological with, "I do believe in god." But when the follow-up question, "How do you know there is a god?" is asked of a Post-Theological, the obvious answer to the query would be, "That wasn't your question."

Another problem agnosticism raises is it leaves more room for trouble than either Post-Theological or theological thought in not allowing for a divine option. This can lead to a moral muddle with no real foundational doctrine of right or wrong. If you consider the two sides of the "evil" argument, religions believe in true good and true evil in the world. Atheists believe that moral truth originates either from man's genetic inclinations or a developed sense of humanity. They do not believe in an objective value of good or evil; there is just man's humanity to man.

Agnostics have no foundational foot in either camp. The agnostic lives in a constant state of theological ambiguity, of not-knowing. As Hitchens puts it, "In just the same way that any democracy is better than any dictatorship, so even the compromise of agnosticism is better than faith. It minimizes the totalitarian temptation, the witless worship of the absolute, and the surrender of reason, that may have led to saintliness but can hardly repay for the harm it has done." But in his argument, Hitchens fails to connect the lack of "totalitarian temptation" to dogma dismissively referring to religion as the "surrender of reason" and "witless worship of the absolute." With statements like those it is no wonder atheism has developed a troubled reputation.

Being Post-Theological means that you may not know, but you believe. You have an unshakeable belief that there is something or someone at the cosmological controls, but you can't posit anything more. This is based on belief, not knowledge or proof. We, the Post-Theological, take a position. Agnosticism does not take a side in the god-argument and because of that, like atheism, still leaves many searching for purpose.

9

POST-THEOLOGICAL AND EASTERN RELIGIONS

"If you meet the Buddha on the road, kill him!"
Ancient Zen aphorism

I have a close friend who was raised in China and is a practicing buddhist. Having extensive life experiences in both western and eastern cultures gives her an interesting perspective on the West's religious outlook. She has a funny fascination with westerners regarding Eastern thought. Living in Seattle, she finds it amusing to see non-Asians studying, learning, and embracing buddhism as an answer to life's stresses and problems. It puzzles her that so many friends and family flock to Eastern religious figures like the Dalai Lama, buying up buddhist and hindu icons, and meditating in local ashrams and prayer rooms. Seattle is like that; alternative, granola, spiritual. To quote my Asian friend, "It's like you people think we don't have any problems because we're buddhists. Some of the most screwed-up people I've ever met are devout followers of the Buddha. Sheesh!" I see her point.

While Asian religions may be less dogmatic and rule-based, they still a rule base common to western monotheisms. There are many "rules" and "right ways" that, when violated, result in offenders' punishment. Different from the western you-did-this-so-you-get-that sort of punishment logic, it is more of a you-did-this-so-you-become-that divine algorithm. But still, it follows the same formula.

But before we dig deeper, a short and admitted simplistic history lesson to inform the argument. Hinduism, the oldest of Eastern religions, is henotheistic in that it has a devotion to one god (Brahma) but accepts the existence of others. It predates the christian idea of a trinity with Brahma (creator), Vishnu (sustainer), and Shiva (destroyer), making up the divine trio. Hinduism was also the origin, as far as we can tell, of the circular version of time instead of the western linear concept. The idea of rebirth up or down the food-chain originated in hindu, and while the foundational tenets are monotheistic, hindus believe that this one god can take many forms. Buddhism, which is descended from hinduism, is non-theistic, rejecting the idea of a creator deity. Even the Buddha is not a god; he is a teacher. The goal of buddhists, like those of hindus, is to escape the circle of painful existence, to reach nirvana. The buddhists concepts of dharma (the "right way" of living) and karma (the good and bad actions that determine our next life) are taken directly from its hindu origins.

Shinto, a Japanese creed, is an amalgamation of traditional Japanese beliefs and buddhism. More akin to animism, shinto infuses inanimate objects and non-sentient organisms with spirituality in the form of divine spirits. And because of the Japanese cultural emphasis on ritual, it has many rites used to protect its believers from evil spirits and attract good ones.

Taoism has two differing components, philosophical and religious. Both are informed by founding text The Tao Te Ching ascribed to the ancient writer Lao Tzu and, like buddhism, are non-theistic. Closely aligned with Post-Theological beliefs, taoism is perhaps the least dogmatic religion/philosophy with almost no set of exclusionary clauses and no godhead. The ultimate spiritual goal of taoism is to enjoy life as it is encountered, to "participate joyfully in the sorrows of life." Similar to Post-Theological beliefs, taoists refrain from attempts to define god. The closest concept would be the "tao" or right way, which informs and guides life.

All Eastern religions have fundamental and significant differences from the major monotheisms of judaism, christianity, and islam. One of the most important differences is the believer's relationship with god. Western monotheisms believe god has a personal interest in the actions and mis-actions of man. Eastern religions do not believe in an intervening godhead focused on human deeds. There is no invisible man in the sky, keeping a scorecard of your life.

The main incentive program of Eastern religions is karma. Both karma and dharma, the words taken originally from hindu Sanskrit, apply to the right livelihood. You can think of karma as the points awarded or deducted based on your actions and Dharma as the rules for playing the game. You live a "good" life in accordance with dharma adding good karma or subtracting bad karma to your celestial scorecard.

Both hindu and buddhist doctrine has the idea of samsara (buddhist) or maya (hindu) which roughly translated means that the material world is an illusion, that all we experience is a "veil" which obscures true reality. The goal is to transcend this life/ veil to reach a higher level of being and ultimately nirvana. You transcend this life of pain by understanding the Fourth Truths of the Buddha.

The First Truth is that life is suffering. Once you accept this, it should make things easier, and you can move onto the next Truth. The Second Truth is that all suffering comes from our desires or craving for things outside of ourselves. The world with all its pains and pleasures, ultimately lead to our unhappiness. The Third Truth is that it is possible to be released from suffering if you live by the guidance provided by the Fourth Truth, the eight-fold path of Right Livelihood. It's kind of an alternative approach to monotheisms list of dos and don'ts, but not that different when you consider the core message.

Buddhism's good/bad karma philosophy/theology is another take on the causality premise similar to western monotheism. As you live your life, you accrue good or bad karma based on your deeds and actions. Depending on how much good or bad karma you've accrued by the end of your life, you move up or down the food chain; that the things you do will determine your next life. For example, if you treat women poorly in this life, you will likely be reborn as a woman. If you commit crimes against animals, you will be punished by being reincarnated lower on the food chain. There are a number of sacred buddhist texts that predict the actual punishment or reward you will receive in your next life based on your deeds in this life.

The problem with the idea of rebirth and karma is that it is both fatalistic and deterministic. Even though you cannot "re-call" the bad or good things you did in your last life, you are still responsible for them. This makes the bad things that happen to you and the unfortunate situations you find yourself in the result of decisions you can neither remember nor control leaving believers with no recourse to their fate.

I had a good friend who was a devout Japanese zen buddhist. After being diagnosed with inoperable stomach cancer, she went to Japan to see a renowned spiritual healer. While the "healer" could do nothing to treat the cancer, she thought seeing him might ease her transition into the next life. In the end, his counseling and advice actually made her transition much, much more difficult.

After a short conversation about my friend's life up until her fatal diagnosis, this "spiritual" man proclaimed her fear of being poor in her last life and led to her developing the fatal ailment in this life. He told her that if she had accepted that she had no control over being rich or poor when she was younger, she might have avoided cancer. This is not only a perfect example of the fatalistic view of buddhism; it is evil and cruel. Contracting a life-threatening disease has many complex biological and environmental factors and blaming a person facing imminent death that she caused her own cancer is a horrible, inhuman act. (We can only hope that this holy man will be reincarnated as an ass. Or maybe he already has.) How can a person be responsible for their own unhappiness or health when they cannot remember who or what you were in a previous life? How can a past life you cannot even remember, or re-call have such devastating consequences in your life?

And how dare anyone tell you that you brought a terminal diagnosis on yourself, especially when facing an existential crisis. How incredibly thoughtless and narcissistic to believe that you can see into people's past lives and condemn their actions and lives in the present.

The very buddhist concept of reincarnation and relegation to other forms of life is another attempt to explain the unexplainable. The idea of gaining or losing cosmic points in a sort of "spiritual materialism" game seems in direct conflict with buddhist teachings – like living in an existential arcade and earning tickets for over-priced items and like major monotheisms, buddhists, hindus, and other Eastern believers are not exactly motivated by humanistic principles to be good people. They do good in fear of being relegated to a dung beetle's trials in the next life in an attempt to win enough points to move up to a higher level of existence (and in case you didn't know, the hindu justification for its brutal and unfair caste system).

Though many westerners are attracted to Eastern religions because of their freshness and egalitarian teachings relative to stale and authoritative western religions, they often realize that even eastern theologic/philosophic belief systems have their own version of the afterlife, rituals regarding birth and death based on aged religious thought and godhead(s) to be worshipped in their statu-ed temples.

After studing buddhism for many years, it occurred to me that there is something subtle about eastern philosophies that rub me the wrong way. In essence, buddhism rejects the most basic foundation of being human, emotion.

The buddhist philosophy of "detachment" is the belief that the world and its pain is something to leave behind. Buddhists believe that there are good emotions and bad emotions. The "good emotions" like joy, love, and compassion are revered and encouraged, as long as you don't overdo them. Showing too much joy or glee is considered rude and inappropriate. Anger, grief, and pain are viewed as things to be avoided by detaching from earthly desires. A great buddhist writer once said, "Anger is the greatest evil; patient forbearance is the greatest austerity." But as we know from modern psychology, suppressed anger can lead to depression, anxiety, and other somatic ailments if not addressed. Anger, fear, and hatred are more than frowned upon in Asian society, and people are encouraged to repress these very human emotions, especially in public. Showing any kind of extreme emotion is one way to lose face and face the shame of your peers. This results in the social stigma for any Asian seeking help in the form of psychotherapy or medication.

Studies show the tendency for Asians to see emotional stress as a physical ailment. As a result, Asian cultures shun counseling and therapy as unnecessary and shameful. Whereas in the West, we view on addiction as a mental health issue to be dealt with in rehab or with familial and community support. Asian culture's sensitivity to communal shame keeps many from seeking help to process emotions.

One reason there are more than 1.5 million self-proclaimed buddhists in the US is exactly because the "barriers to entry" are very low for anyone wanting to become a buddhist. You simply go to a temple, of which there are more and more in the US, and declare to your friends and family that you are a convert to the 6th largest religion (about 470 million adherents) in the world.

For me, it seems just too damn easy to profess yourself as having reached "enlightenment" without having to prove any measurable criteria. I had a friend who proclaimed herself enlightened even though she could not hold down a job, had two children who were highly anxious and depressed, and she routinely neglected to pay for parking tickets until she was arrested. It is difficult to equate this type of behavior to a Bodhisattva (an enlightened person who chooses to stay on earth to help others attain nirvana).

Most other religions have a much higher bar. A Seattle friend of mine became a follower of the Talmud in his 60s (late on-set Judaism). His initiation into that group was much more difficult. After an extensive study of the Talmud and other jewish writings he had to undergo an evaluation by a Beit Dem or jewish court. Once he passed that hurdle, his final approval was not complete until his ritual bath or mikveh and given his hebrew name. (Luckily, he was already circumcised as that might have been a deal-breaker). Even though he was appropriating an ancient and serious theology late in life, the initiation took more effort than he expected. A decidedly more difficult road than simply waking up one morning and declaring yourself buddhist.

And despite the increased appropriation of eastern religions by western society, it might be good for some to know that many monks are convicted criminals. To reduce prison overcrowding and save money, it is common for a judge to assign time in a temple as a punishment for misdemeanors and even felonies. (Similar as it was for young men in the US to escape incarceration with military service. And that didn't do wonders to improve the quality of the ranks of American service members).

In February of 2019, the Thai police cracked down on the Subhan Buri temple in Bangkok in an attempt to find and arrest criminal monks accused of, among other things, murder and sexual harassment. The Thai government has a special unit whose job is to "sweep temples clean by further unmasking criminals-turned-monks nationwide." More of the contemporary patina has worn off Eastern religions as the West is regularly exposed to saffron-robed monks engaging in armed conflict. With YouTube videos of buddhists clashing with other religions that threaten to occupy the spaces and lands they feel are theirs by tradition, we are beginning to see that perhaps it is not the answer to all our problems.

But we can be happy that at least buddhism doesn't have the apocalyptic vision common to major Western theisms. Monotheism's messianic/apocalyptic nature predicts an end-times with a god who decides who wins everlasting bliss and who wins everlasting torture. The winners of this spiritual competition get to spend the rest of their days (?) in the kingdom of god.

There is no equivalent in Eastern theological doctrine. Only by reaching nirvana can human beings break the cycle of birth and rebirth into higher and lower sentience.

While there are occasional death-cults that arise in the east, the numbers of religious zealots trying to initiate the "end-of-days" scenario in the west are legion. From Heaven's Gate to the Jonestown mass suicide to the sad and pointless Branch Davidians mass suicide in Waco, Texas (a splinter group of the Seventh Day Adventists who merrily continue their wild and stupid teachings), all their leaders claimed to have been blessed with the gift of prophecy. David Koresh, the head of the Waco cult and boy who grew up with sexual abuse and alcoholism throughout his young life, claimed that god told him to have sex with a 60-something widow of a former cult leader to produce the new messiah. He led 76 severely misguided people, 25 of whom were children, to their death in the Waco compound firestorm in spite of being a crazed idiot.

Many so-called spiritual gurus end up being alcoholic womanizers who exploit their followers. Some defend their serial exploitation as "wisdom we non-believers just don't understand" even after witnessing them using their special "awareness" to enrich themselves and seduce young women. The messianic and apocalyptic underpinnings of western monotheism of a god who, in the end, will decide the fate of all humanity has prompted too many people to try and initiate the process themselves.

We can be happy that buddhism lack this underlying vision of an end-of-days scenario that finalizes life in an apocalyptic Armageddon. To the eastern mind, the quest for nirvana through the acquisition of good or bad karma is an eternal struggle with no end-point other than your own escape from that struggle. There is no eternal heaven or hell at the end of one's being. There is no answer to the question of what happens once you reach nirvana; escaping the suffering of birth and rebirth seems to be enough. Buddhism does not deny the existence of a creator of the universe, but believers don't seem to find the question interesting. Since all of the material world is samsara anyway, the universe is a hoax, a mask, an experience we must escape. But the question of what lies after this world is not important enough to warrant speculation. Weird, huh?

The ultimate goal is escape. Escaping from the unbearable and painful Ground Hog Day until they "get it right" plays well in a third-world country where life is difficult, and day-to-day existence spans from extreme boredom to constant pain and suffering. Buddhism offers these poor people enough hope to enable them to get up and put one foot in front of the other despite enormous obstacles and bleak or non-existent opportunities. While in the west, many feel grandiose enough to equate their emotional discomforts with third world misery as if this promotion-demotion belief system is a parlor game.

Post-Theological thought rejects the idea of knowing we are reborn while fully embracing the Right-Minded way of buddhist thought. We can conceive that there is a possibility of rebirth, but we can't know that there is a cosmic scorecard that pushes us up or down the ladder of existence. The Noble Truths provide a good and moral way to live life, but to think that we can use it to escape this life's sufferings or increase our joys is simply more dogma – there is no possible way to know this. This is not to propose that buddhism is more of a sham than any other faith. But after the initial Fab Four buddhist epiphanies that went viral in the 1960s, the infatuation for eastern philosophy has topped out as more of a niche religion in the west. Regional differences notwithstanding, like the Northwest's embrace of eastern religions, eastern religion,will never experience widespread adoption in the west. Still, it will remain a source of charlatan expropriation by new age "fakirs" to fill their proprietary pews with spiritual nomads.

The same motivations that drive monotheisms – the desire to know our fate, the need to believe in a theo-cultural morality, the fear of an ambiguous meaning to life – drives eastern religions as well.

Buddhism, for all its good qualities, one of the oldest theologies (450BC) originated as a way to answer the same questions as other religions. How did we get here? Why are we here, and where are we going? For the truly Post-Theological person, these questions have not and will not be answered.

We, the Post-Theological reject that any eastern religion can know what god wants from us or how success in a life after death is impacted by a human set of rules. In the end, the distance between western theological dogma and buddhist philosophy is not that great. For the Post-Theological, living without dogma is as much an alternative to Eastern thought as it is to Western.

10

POST-THEOLOGICAL PURPOSE

"If you have an experience of unconditional love,
that's a spiritual experience ... but it doesn't
tell you anything about the cosmos."
Sam Harris

In Sam Harris's latest book, *Waking Up*, he posits that it isn't necessary to believe in a god to have spiritual experiences. His argument is that being "present" is enough to generate transcendent feelings and experience the wonder and awe at the majesty of the universe. In making this weirdly defensive argument, he uses his own personal moments of wonder as proof that it is possible to have a spiritually fulfilling experience without actually being spiritual. The transcendent stretch Harris seems to be making is a weak attempt to fill a gap that atheism cannot; the lack of purposefulness and wonder many people associate and experience with their religion.

Many people are attracted to atheism, at least at first, by the idea of escaping dogmatic, controlling theism. But the demographics of atheism point to it being the privileged few who make up the bulk of non-believers. According to the Pew Research on Religion and Society, the two main driving factors for atheism is "financial security and education." The research is validated by the fact that most atheists turn out to be white, affluent western men. Being in a first-world economy and society is inextricably linked to rejecting the idea of a godhead. It makes sense in a financially secure world, there are many more choices, including religious options.

But the recent decline in the number of atheists and the growing contempt for New Atheism by their ex-converts points to the failed attempts by their spokespeople (the Four Horsemen, again) to equivocate normal human wonder with religious mystical experience. Theological or religious transcendence is the experience of talking with or feeling one with your god. Ancient ascetics and hermits claimed transcendent and mystical experiences after starving themselves and avoiding human contact for months in harsh environments. Non-theological transcendence is often described as feelings of being "one with the universe" sometimes after drug-induced hallucinations. Regarding the latter, laic or non-religious transcendence emerged in the sixties in the US and became the foundation for many movements, including environmentalism. It was basically harmless because it was based on individual experience and its only dogma was "if it feels good, do it." Religious transcendence is different and used by many ancient writers to explain how the "touch" of god enabled them to understand what he, not she, wants from us.

The rub becomes real when you compare the criteria different religions apply to their proprietary "transcendence." All religions reject the idea that a person who does not believe in their god can still experience the transcendent feelings and wonder typically identified as spiritual. Growing up in a catholic community, I was encouraged to "feel bad" that pagan babies would never have the opportunity to know god in all his "goodness." The good nuns often led us in prayer for those unfortunate souls who could never bask in the wonderment of god's creations because they did not believe. This question is often posed to atheists like Harris, Hitchens, and Dawkins by the religiously smug. They question a viewpoint that would reject the creation of the sky, the moon, the stars, and all the other natural wonders for us to enjoy by a benevolent god. Harris's self-referential attempts to equate secular transcendence with religious transcendence doesn't quite make a feasible argument.

But these theocratic bullies are not just using divine bliss to counter the anti-theist arguments of the New Atheists. What they are saying is that someone who does not believe in *their* god cannot enjoy *their* proprietary divine transcendence. Understanding this rebuke of non-believers reveals the hypocrisy of the question. They are claiming spiritual transcendence for their religious members alone. At their core, christians do not believe that muslims, jews, hindus, or buddhists can experience a divine and transcendent moment if the initiator of the moment is not their christian god.

The idea of looking up at the Milky Way and experiencing the wonder and awe of our physical universe is only valid if we give thanks to Jesus Christ and his Father for creating it. If a muslim looks up and praises Allah for this gift of wonder, then by the christian definition, it is not true transcendence (is there such a thing as false transcendence?). According to islam, if a jew is brought to tears by the birth of his or her child and thanks yahweh, by definition, this is wasted energy. To a christian, if a buddhist monk leaves his body through intense meditation and chanting, this does not bring him closer to the right god.

This is rubbish. All people have the ability, the right, the sentience to experience all kinds of wonderful things, from the deep emotional response to a Shakespeare sonnet to a spark of wonderment from standing next to Michelangelo's David. The idea that a person is given an exclusive license to feelings of wonder and beauty by his own personal god is stupid.

This is the same for the Post-Theological. Being without dogma does not limit our ability to glow in the warmth and wonder of our emotions and our universe. People can still live a fulfilling, joyful, and spiritual life We can experience the transcendent, just like the religious.

Taking the elitist religious argument a step further, they would have you believe that the idea of praying to your god for anything-forgiveness, health, love, or whatever – is folly as well because there are no divine ears to hear your pleas. The prayers you say to *your* god are not valid to *their* god and vice versa. A christian god will never hear the prayers of a muslim, and allah will never hear the prayers of a jew.

In that Post-Theological faith does not allow for the ideation of god/the Unknowable, that doesn't mean there is nothing to live for or even necessarily changes the ways many practice their private religion. Being Post-Theological means that we can never know god, but that doesn't mean we cannot be thankful for the good things that happen in our lives or angry about the bad things. Even accepting that we can never know or ideate a "god" nor know his/her/its intentions doesn't mean we cannot pray or talk to this force.

Praying to a divine source, asking the Unknowable for blessings is not a bad thing as long as we manage our expectations. To think that when our prayers are answered is anything more than synchronicity doesn't hurt anyone – and who knows, maybe our prayers *are* answered. When those of faith pray for something and receive it, they thank their god. When they pray for something and get no "response," then god must have a mysterious reason for denying their request – a theological, Bizzaro-Catch-22. Traditional religions give their god a pass from any accountability for his response or lack thereof to their prayers. Their god is right, whether he does something good, bad, or indifferent.

Being Post-Theological is a more pragmatic and useful faith because it does not rely on an external invisible being to direct our lives. While many may think that the idea of asking god for personal favors is benign or even good, it can have some truly evil consequences when this faith is absolute and uncompromising.

A family in our neighborhood had a son who died from cancer at the age of twenty-one. His parents did everything possible to make him healthy again, searching for medical and spiritual cures, but the cards were not in his favor. Towards the end of his illness, his parents took him to Lourdes and the Vatican in a desperate attempt to convince god to heal him. They prayed over him constantly in an attempt to beat back the spread of this horrible disease; they were unflinching in their belief that the hand of god might actually step in to extend his life.

Until he didn't.

Many atheists would brand his parents as fools. That asking an invisible man in the clouds to miraculously cure their son is naïve and childish. I've witnessed atheists dismissing truly human misery as brought on by attachment to religious beliefs. Muslims would denounce their efforts as misguided because they put the hopes of a healthy son into the hands of the wrong god; that the god of islam is the only legitimate source of divine intervention in a tragic situation like this. Buddhists would tell them to examine their present and past lives to find the origins of their son's and suffering.

As a Post-Theological, I see this boy's parents' desperate acts as the embodiment of love and humanity. A parent's pain for their dying child is universal and transcendent of religion; it is a human tragedy. I do not judge his parent's actions or their attempts to stave off their son's pain and death. I do not dismiss their agony as caused by stupid religious attachments. I see it as another example of the great human story.

I *do* denounce the promises their faith made to them about the power and attention their god gives to the faithful. I denounce the so-called interpreters of god's word and their minions of perpetrators spreading the "good" word. It is disgraceful and evil, and they should be ashamed of themselves for putting so many people through so much pain. Being brought up and fed a spiritual diet of these same false promises and deluded dogmas created the belief that we can expect more from our god than we should. Raised on a steady diet of belief in god's goodness and mercy, I was told to pray to him for relief from all physical and emotional pain. He never bothered to intervene, but I was encouraged all the same by nuns and clergy to pray harder for god's help.

The Post-Theological believe prayer is not a bad thing. Having an unshakable belief that some/thing/one is at the controls means we can pray and talk to this entity. Faith, even Post-Theological faith, can be comforting. Self-sacrifice is not a bad thing. The transcendent idea of love and caring for your family and mankind is not a bad thing. And while asceticism doesn't really add anything to the world, it isn't really a bad thing.

The same is true for meditation. Chanting to your idea of a god is fine for buddhists, christians, and muslims as much as it is for the Post-Theological. There are proven medical reasons for chanting and evidence that it reduces stress and improves concentration. Being Post-Theological doesn't negate any of this, nor does it change the impact of spiritual prayer and chanting. Post-Theological thought frees us from the religious dogma that controls our lives and purpose. Unlike traditional monotheisms, Post-Theological faith accepts that our god is not a personal god that directly answers or fails to answer our prayers based on his willy-nilly plan for our life; it free us from this totalitarian, controlling belief system. Accepting that it is impossible to know or intuit god's desire leaves us free from the need to kowtow to our version of a supreme being.

11

Post-Theological Enlightenment

> "We hold these truths to be self-evident, that all men are
> created equal, that they are endowed by their Creator
> with certain unalienable Rights, that among these
> are Life, Liberty and the Pursuit of Happiness."
> A proclamation of Enlightened Men

Is it possible to live in a world without religious dogma and still create a moral, civilized society? We do not know...

... yet.

Our world has been so ingrained with the idea that religion is the only true source of morality that it will take some time to figure this all out. The crucial question is whether humanity can create a world with a morality that is defendable, grounded in humanistic principles, and attractive enough to people and governments to become a basis for global human rights.

The answer is that it already has.

But before we go there, we must address the idea of "objective morality." Objective Morality is the belief that certain moral truths exist independent of human opinion and dialogue. This is the view that the universe has an inherent moral foundation, and if we have can discern it we create a noble society.

There are two competing views of "objective" morality. The first is based on religious dogma. All religions claim that *their* proprietary set of god-inspired rules and doctrine is unquestionable, righteous and objective. People like the self-appointed president of the fake-university, Dennis Prager, equates atheism with moral decay while defending Donald Trump, perhaps the most amoral person ever to hold high office. Prager's "objective morality" is based on his own faith and cannot be separated from it. He refers to it as universal objective morality even though the only version he allows for is based on his version of the Bible.

Prager's side of the argument is divisive and the cause of so many unnecessary and brutal acts. Based on ancient beliefs, every modern religion's foundational tomes justify killing homosexuals, defiling women, and murdering non-believers. And even though many religious will point out that the idea of murdering another infidel is abhorrent, it doesn't keep many or most from damning gays and non-believers to eternal hell.

The other side of the equation is the idea of moral relativism. Moral relativists claim that no one ethical system is better than another. They believe that no culture has the right to impose its cultural mores on another, that no society walks a morally superior road. For mostly ideological reasons, some public figures who shall remain nameless (Bill O'Reilly) equate atheistic ideas with moral relativism. But that is mostly grandstanding in support of their own brand of self-righteousness (Is it bad being self-righteous if I am right?)

But these thought-Nazis have it wrong and show willful ignorance in order to promote their brand of righteousness. It is clear that atheists are not moral relativists when more thought is given to their beliefs. Most atheists are well-meaning people who love their families, friends, and communities. Painting all atheists as immoral reprobates only shows the ignorance of people like the Bill O'Reilly's and Dennis Prager's of the world.

However, the dilemma atheist face illustrates the challenges of staking a claim to an alternative moral foundation other than religion. Atheists struggle to create a space between religious morality and moral relativism that can be logically defended. Sam Harris is currently trying to create a defense of moral objectivity using evolutionary biology and neuropsychology. He hopes that studies of the brain will show that moral decisions have a different brain activity than immoral activities. Perhaps this will bear fruit, but it is not likely to reverse the decline in the New Atheists' popularity.

As the New Atheists argue with the Theological for a basis of human morality, human society's evolution provides a clear historical perspective that validates human moral evolution claims. Sociologists make a strong argument that human morals have evolved despite, and not because of, theist and anti-theistic dogma. Darwin's thesis, "I fully subscribe to the judgment of those writers who maintain that of all the differences between man and the lower animals, the moral sense or conscience is by far the most important," is difficult to prove as a golden rule. Morality may be linked to evolution, but the conflicting studies will need more evolutional time to make a convincing argument one way or the other.

But while this tension between the two perspectives of morality may one day be settled, it seems that there is something to be said for a type of moral truth that exists already in situ. It is difficult to deny that an easily observable human morality exists today regardless of its origins and evolution.

Contemporary societies believe that murdering a child is immoral, but the Spartans and Romans regularly practiced infanticide. Human sacrifice was common in many early civilizations, mostly to appease their gods, but any culture that would attempt this practice now would become a global pariah. (Let's hope.) Even with the tolerance of other cultures, there are examples of truly "good" and truly "bad" societies and organizations. While

Nazism is an easy target, we can also point to aspects of other current societies that can be judged as objectively "bad," including repressive African regimes and Qatar's smothering society.

As a global species, for the most part, we have reached a mutual abhorrence for slavery, both physical and sexual. It isn't that there aren't examples of sexual and physical slavery to be found in many countries today, but most nations agree that this is wrong, moving to make it illegal and deploying intentional efforts to limit and eliminate this scourge. But, like Qatar's sponsorship laws, which de-facto institutionalize slavery, this evil still exists. Today, agricultural slavery is outlawed and rare, but a very familiar form of slavery can be observed in the nail salons and car washes in free countries like the UK. The 2019 Global Slavery Index highlights the issue and is viewed by proponents as key to progress, but those who fall at the bottom of the Freedom from Slavery list, including North Korea, Russia, and Somalia, continue to attack its credibility. Things like the Global Slavery Index point to an evolving sense of morality and moral truth based on our species' experience and emotional development. Despite setbacks and even long periods of immorality, the world has come a long way in making the thoughts and ideas of the Enlightenment part of human development. And even though many have forgotten the impact of the Age of Reason (1685 – 1815), its influence is not only recognizable today but continues to guide our species' development and clearly evident in many recent and not so recent moral standards and codes.

Wikipedia states, "The Enlightenment was a period of time in which cultural and intellectual forces in Western Europe emphasized reason, analysis and the individual rather than traditional lines of authority. Politically, the age is distinguished by economic liberty, republicanism, and religious tolerance, as clearly expressed in the United States Declaration of Independence. Attempts to reconcile science and religion resulted in a rejection of prophecy miracle and revealed religion, resulting in an inclination toward deism among some major political leaders of the age. American republicanism emphasized consent of the government, riddance of aristocracy, and fear of corruption."

After the horror of World War II, the world came together prompted by the inhumanity of the Nazi and Japanese regimes. With this particular war being the closest thing to a justified conflict between nihilistic and humanistic ideologies, the United Nations, a distinctly global and secular organization, identified a set of morals laid out in the UN Declaration of Human Rights established in 1948 (Guinness Book of World Records identifies it as the most translated document in the history of the world).

The term Declaration was used to recognize the US Declaration of Independence's success in creating a secular and representative society. In this Enlightened document, the signing governments agreed to secure the universal recognition of a set of human rights. Though not a legally binding document, the UN Declaration was adopted in 1948 and has had a significant impact on many national constitutions. It has also been incorporated into a growing number of national and international laws and treaties protecting and promoting human rights. And while not perfect, it contains some of the basic tenets of an international, humanistic and moral code.

The Declaration of Human Rights avers four basic human freedoms: freedom of speech, freedom of religion, freedom from fear, and freedom from want. The Charter "reaffirmed faith in fundamental human rights and the dignity and worth of the human person." It committed all member states to promote "universal respect for, and observance of, human rights and fundamental freedoms for all without distinction of race, sex, language, or religion."

Regardless of whether all people or governments accept it, the Declaration codifies and communicates a set of universal moral truths. It reinforces the idea that men and women are intellectually, economically, politically, and morally equal and should be treated that way. This is not to say they are the same. (Some literalistic idiots reject it based on the argument that it does not clearly express the biological differences between a man and a woman.) Assumed in the document is that while different physiologically and therefore better at some things than their opposite sex (men at developing prostate problems, women at gestating fetuses), both genders are of equal worth.

Its proclaimed freedom of religion – this "moral truth" – is as much aimed at theocratic governing models as autocratic ones that repress religious choices and accept alternative dogma. In it is assumed that secular institutions, especially governments, work better than theocracies or dictatorial regimes. Democratic, representative secular governments make better, more informed, and more inclusive decisions about the societies they oversee. Freedom from authoritarian regimes and the right of one person/ one vote is an endpoint of enlightened human development and crucial to our species' survival.

Problems are too varied and solutions too complex to allow anything less than democratic free speech to inform and propel political, social, and economic decision-making. Human freedom to pursue a socially responsible, purposeful life is critical to our species' flourishing and future. Today's weapons in the fight against man's inhumanity to man are the secular and egalitarian principles critical to our survival.

We cannot take these truths for granted. We must remain on our guard as the fight to integrate religion into politics continues at the supra-national level of organizations like the United Nations even today. Recent attempts by muslim nations to introduce drafts outlawing criticism of the Qur'an and prevent proposals declaring equal women's rights are cynical and repressive. The idea that one religion can impose its dogma on global society is abhorrent to any free-thinking man or woman and should be fought both tooth and nail. Traditional eastern bloc countries

STEVE REILLY

promote theories and legislation aimed at undoing the work of
free and liberal societies.

On another front, modern-day theologians argue that our societies are experiencing a breakdown in morality due to the absence of theological values incorporated into national principles.
This, of course, is self-serving. They are correct to aver that today's moral code is based on early religious enlightenment, but
in those times, the only human life that was "sacred" was that of
the believers – not pagans or heathens. (Talk to a descendant of
the Native American nation, if you can find one.)

Arguably, ancient theologies provided a behavioral code that
prevented people of the same beliefs from slaughtering each
other. But if you found yourself outside the religious "clique,"
you were more likely to be tortured and killed for being contrary.
Religion may have been the beginning of moral authority, but we
have since outgrown the theological model.

Religion used and uses intelligent design in defense of an
almighty creator. In defense of his faith's particular dogma Dr.
William Lane Craig, a theologian and biblical scholar, argues
that if one of the forces/laws of nature shifted by an incredibly
small amount, life would not be able to exist or flourish in this
universe. He and his fellow believers are correct, of course, about
the physics, but that doesn't prove anything. Making the jump
from a delicately balanced and incredibly fortuitous location in
the galaxy to the design of a benevolent creator is ridiculous unless you also blame the unfortunate and random misfortunes
on the same god. Asking us to believe the god who intentionally
placed the earth at the exact spot between the sun and the rest
of space so that a green planet could thrive mistakenly put us in
a world that regularly delivers devastation to its inhabitants is a
stretch too far.

Anti-theists point out that if creation was a divine act, then
god made a mess of it. The late, great Christopher Hitchens
pointed out that since our species spent the first ten thousand

years of existence in a life that was brutal, savage, painful, and mercifully short, the lord must have been a bit slow on the uptake. It took tens of thousands of years for humanity to drag itself out of the tar pits and rain forests to begin to build cities and escape a brutish existence.

The evangelicals would want us to believe man was created just as he is today without considering that pre-man struggled against horrific dangers and bewildering natural calamities. But regardless of whether this finely balanced universal equation was created by a deity interested in our own personal survival or it all happened by chance, it is miraculous. Regardless of whether our existence is a gift from an all-knowing creature or an error in cosmic rounding, the gift of life enables us to live, learn, create, discover and watch the English Premier League!

This makes life, all life, incredibly... hmmm, looking for a word here.

Sacred is not the proper word; too much theological baggage. Logical is another loaded word, but the atheists will like it. The correct word is precious. Earth's cosmic lottery win of location, carbon, electromagnetic forces, and distance from a friendly star makes life – not just human life but all life – precious. If only for that fact that we are a very, very tiny speck in an immeasurable universe that emerged from the prehistoric ooze to live, love, and even hate, makes every life a precious gift to the universe.

We don't need theism or antitheism to tell us that. We experience it every day in our wonderful, miraculous, and very human world. Keep in mind that the closest possible sentient life form to our planet is more than one hundred million light-years away – if it exists at all. This makes our sentience a cosmic gift of extraordinary proportions.

And the more sentient the life, the more precious it is. While members of the jains religion carry a brush to sweep away any tiny insect or animal they might inadvertently rub out with a simple step, most of humanity would agree that stepping on an ant is not the same as murdering a person. In theory, we could argue that ants feel pain in the same way a higher form of life like a cat, cow, or person does, but the odds of making a universally agreed upon matrix identifying the degree of sentience based on descending complexity of life forms is probably not in the cards. We can leave it with the idea that life, all life, is precious, but we've got to eat.

At the personal level, the lives of people special to us make the argument for an objective value of life even stronger. Whether it is the instantaneous love generated by your child's birth or the feelings we have for family and friends, humans have an inherent desire to experience and extend their own lives and the lives of their loved ones. Living and loving make the preservation of human life precious. This ability to engage and connect with loved ones transcends borders, religions, and politics. It has become, if not always was, an inherent human trait and moral truth. Having compassion for other members of our species is as human as we can be.

As for moral relativism, most cultures define the lack of human compassion as a sickness and a personality disorder; we call them sociopaths or psychopaths. So, how can we identify these outliers of human morality but be reluctant to define human empathy, compassion, and caring as normative human behavior?

Some will ask how this squares with the ubiquitous cruelty, murder, and mayhem we regularly inflict on our fellow man. Yes, we slaughter hundreds, even thousands, of our kind by the day, but that doesn't deter us from trying to make a better world so our children can also experience the joys we treasure. We attempt this even knowing that they will undoubtedly experience great suffering and pain. This is what it means to be human. Think about it, all love stories end in a tragedy, yet we continue to love.

But if as a species, we can agree that life – all life – is precious, not for religious or neuro-scientific reasons but for the sheer joy of being alive against incredibly bad universal odds, then perhaps we can begin to build a world free of religious dogma. To accomplish this, we/the Post-Theological must stand up for human moral truth. We must hold all organizations, governments, churches, individuals, and groups accountable for violating this universal code of human rights.

We must speak out.

We have the right and the duty to speak out against horrific acts justified by barely post-hominid writings. We should speak out against every example of pedantic elitism from the jehovah's witnesses that visit our door proselytizing their proprietary dogma to the imam who condemns homosexuals because his god says they are evil.

We must fight.

As the Post-Theological, we will fight and rail against the hasidim who refuse to sit next to a woman, against mormons who believe polygamy is a gift from god, against muslins who refuse to let women participate in their society, and against a pope that allows rapists and their protectors to live peaceful lives behind Vatican walls.

We must take a stand.

We cannot be Post-Theological without standing against the suppression of free speech, the repression of women, the condemnation of homosexuality, and the hypocrisy of mullahs, priests, rabbis, preachers, and evangelicals. We are done letting the smug religious elite steal our world, our truth, and our lives.

We must not tolerate.

As the Post-Theological, we see no distinction between the catholic priest that rapes a young boy and a muslim who rapes his wife. We see no difference between a government that represses its people and a hindu who represses his children. We see no difference between a religion that encourages female genital mutilation and one that discourages female education. There is no sliding scale of morality.

We are moral.

We know right from wrong. We know that humans have a right to be free, to be educated, and to pursue happiness. Whether it is a religion, a government, a political party, or a financial entity that restricts or represses these rights, we will fight them.

We know.

We know that repressing, torturing, or killing any human being is wrong. We know that governments, churches, and regimes that obscure the truth must be brought to justice. We know that it is wrong to take away people's right to speak freely and to be free of suppression and repression. We know it is wrong to deny people the opportunity to learn, eat, and be happy.

We will act.

And for those who do these evil acts, we will bear witness to their inhumanity. We will reveal their hypocrisy; we will pull back the curtains of their lies and make their travesties public.

This is our right; this is our duty; this is our mandate.

We are the Post-Theological. Bring it on.

ABOUT THE AUTHOR

Steve is a writer and thinker who retired to Thailand to follow his dream, surfing. You can find him at the beach most days writing, carving waves and eating delicious Thai meals. He would very much enjoy any feedback. His email is stephenjosephreilly@gmail.com.

No hate mail, please. Remember that *your* god is watching.

Made in the USA
Coppell, TX
31 January 2021

49110682R00080